The heart

is a rough black stone.

A bit of star-stuff,

sooty and smoky,

scorched and burn't on its long fall to earth.

The Star of Opening

A Morningstar Mystery School Anthology

**The Star of Opening:
A Morningstar Mystery School Anthology**

Edited by Anthony Rella and Kathy Nance
Published by Solar Cross Publishing / LVX/NOX
All work herein is the property of its respective creators.

Copyright © 2015
Morningstar Mystery School
all rights reserved

Cover Design © 2015
T. Thorn Coyle

Cover Image:
StarGoddess © Allyson Ramage

This book, or parts thereof, may not be reproduced in any form without permission. This book is licensed for your personal enjoyment only. All rights reserved.

ISBN-13: 978-0692387658 (trade paperback)
ISBN-10: 069238765X (trade paperback)

Table of Contents

Foreword *by T. Thorn Coyle* 1
Preface *by Anthony Rella* 5

~ Praxis ~

Integration Poem *by Lyssa Heartsong*
Prayers for Daily Pratice *by Litha* 9
Establishing a Daily Practice *by Nikolai* 15
Gratitude: A Meditation and Paean *by Kevin Faulker* 29
O, Death—Meditations on Life's Impermanence
   by Rynn Fox 37
Entering the Temple of the Morningstar:
   For Those Who Fear "Astral Rejection"
   by Fortuna 53
Pagan Values *by Ealasaid A. Haas* 61
Embodiment: Ethics and Episteme
   by Kevin Faulkner 77
The Stillness About Which the World Spins
   by Anthony Rella 91

⌒ Gnosis ⌒

Dragon *by Sean McMahon*

Presence *by Elfin* 103

Dark Heart *by Elfin* 105

Death, Remembrance, and Love *by Rynn Fox* 111

The Hinges *by Litha* 119

Demons, Dreams, and Visions:
    Connecting Morningstar and Shamanic Work
    by Annette Rath-Beckmann 131

#1–9 *by Sophia Bonnie Wodin* 141

Pronounced *by Brian C* 147

Bridghid 2013 *by Sophia Bonnie Wodin* 153

Fragment: Godsoul to Me *by Ariana Dawnhawk* 155

My Demon, My Self *by Kathy Nance* 157

The Merkabah *by Sophia Bonnie Wodin* 165

Contributor Biographies 169

Foreword

The definition of desire is to follow a star.

In Morningstar Mystery School, we follow the star that marks the space between night and day. We seek that which dawns within us, spreading brilliance to the world.

Many years ago, I was given a precious gift. A teacher of mine was about to move across the country and said "Why don't you student teach my final class with me?" I had never thought of teaching before. I was in a dance troupe at the time, and was writing and working odd jobs to support my various creative pursuits. But the thought of working with this teacher on a six-week class seemed intriguing.

In the middle of the first night's class, I thought: "This is revolutionary!" Though I had felt the changes in myself from studying, I'd never put it together that teaching helped turn people's worlds inside out and upside down, disturbing the status quo and offering an opening for change…and that I might help facilitate this.

That was more than twenty years ago. I've been learning how to teach ever since. And I've continued learning how to learn. Morningstar Mystery School is the product and the process of all these years.

The people whose words you will read in this anthology are dedicated. Some of them have left the school since this writing—taking the work of Morningstar out into the world—and are using their experience as priests, parents, artists, and as teachers themselves. Some are doing all of that while remaining within the school. The work shines through us all. We all teach. We all continue to learn.

In Morningstar, we may have theories, some even rooted in theologies, but the primary focus of Morningstar Mystery School is gnosis via praxis.

As long as we keep practicing, there is always a chance to learn. Every person whose words are held within these pages is someone who both seeks and who has found.

No one here has given up, no matter how hard things sometimes seem. The words here are insights into their practice, their dedication, their hard-won knowledge and their open hearts. I value these words. But what I really value are the lives that shine behind them.

When a group is dedicated to practice, even when a person leaves the group the connection continues as long as the practice remains.

Foreword

I'm grateful to the people in this anthology. Grateful to the editors of this collection. Grateful to all who have taught me on this way.

We inquire. We practice. We seek the ways that light shines through the fertile darkness, and see how darkness embraces the burgeoning light.

Blessed be our brilliance.

– T. Thorn Coyle

Preface

Under the Waxing Crescent of July 2009, T. Thorn Coyle sent an announcement to her long-term students, formally announcing that "Morningstar Mystery School shall cease to be a school of Feri and shall instead become its own school." Up until this point, many of us studying with her had begun by way of her two-and-a-quarter-year trainings in her particular iteration of Feri tradition, but she had already begun hinting to some of her students that the Work was transforming into something different. "My roots remain in Feri," she wrote in her letter, "but they are also in Gurdjieff and Sufism. My influences are of the Craft, but they are also of Kabbalah, Buddhism, Hinduism, Thelema and mysticism of all traditions."

As of this writing, students of Morningstar live in disparate locations across North America and Europe. We collaborate via an Internet forum, checking in about our overall Work and working on pieces of homework or teachings offered to us by Thorn, our God Souls, the Gods, and other students. We seek to become fully ourselves and step into what is called "the Work of this God." The foundation and fuel of this work is spiritual practice. We have many beliefs and ideas about the nature of our souls, the Gods, and magic, and we have had many vigorous conversations about all of these topics.

Morningstar Mystery School continues to evolve. Each student's Work brings new flavors, ideas, forms and potentials to the whole. There have been many students whose souls have touched and contributed to Morningstar Mystery School, many who are leaders and devout participants in their own communities and traditions. Students participate for as long as the school feeds their own Work, which might range from a few months to several years.

This anthology is an opportunity to capture the thinking, contemplation, and deep soul work that has blossomed from these remarkable students through their connection to Morningstar. I thank each person who has ever been a part of the school, with whom I have been blessed to study. I thank Thorn for her continued guidance, inspiration, and integrity.

Whether you are curious about Morningstar, dedicated to your tradition, or seeking your path, I hope you will find something in this anthology that feeds your Work.

– Anthony Rella

~ *Praxis* ~

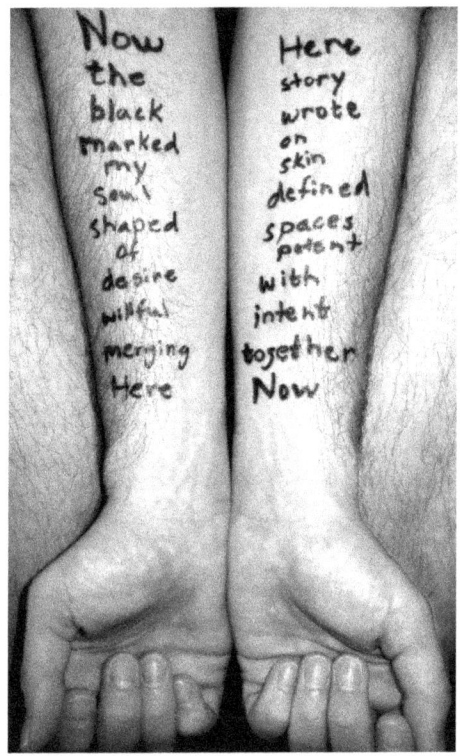

Integration Poem

by Lyssa Heartsong

Prayers for Daily Practice

by Litha

I: Morning Prayer

Mother of wisdom, the breath and the flame,
Let your light move through me.
May I see clearly.

Mother of compassion, the chalice and star,
Let your love move through me.
Let my heart be open.

Mother of spirit, the cauldron of souls,
Come into my centre.
Let my will be yours.
By all that is above me, by all that lies below,

By the breath and the flame, the chalice and star,
Let all evil be banished,

Ill will be transformed.
May I do no harm.

By all that is above me, by all the lies below,
And by the one sound of Her many names,
I dedicate myself to this Earth
And Her purposes.

Blessed be.

II: Pentacle Prayer

With thanks to Thorn, Victor, Cora, Starhawk and many others in the lineage of my witchcraft.

Sex — I claim the life force that is me.
Pride — I know my place in the multiverse.
Self — Who is this flower above me?
Power — I stand at the Centre of my own life, and reach for its circumference.
Passion — I live unconditionally.

Love — I give and I receive.
Law — I live with integrity.
Knowledge — I know myself in all my parts.
Liberty — I act freely and accurately in every moment.
Wisdom — I am that which is attained at the end of desire.

Commitment — I give my word.
Honour — I live by my word.
Truth — I am the work of this god.
Strength — I am the priestess of my life.
Compassion — I see myself in everything, and so I offer kindness.

By all of these, I live my life.
Blessed be.

III: Compassion Prayer

    And did you come, little one,
    Into this life with both eyes open?
    Did you come ready to hear
    All that would be said?
    Did you know, did you fear
    The pain of rough hands,
    Enraged, upon your body
    Even before you were born?

    I think not.

    Believe me, life is meant to be kinder than this.

    Believe me.

IV: Evening Prayer

In the name of Pan, his flute, his lute.
By hallowed hare, by snake, by bear.
For the garden in the moonlight,
And the beauty of each blooming rose it holds,
We offer this:

The wondrous wealth of our sacred hearts
As service, as sacrifice,
As the only authority we hold.

V: Dreamtime Chant

A far shore calls to me, and I must go.
All boats take me there, fast or slow.
I call upon Mystery to guide me as I row.

A far shore calls to me, and I must go.

VI: Prayer Before Sunrise

In morning, as morning, as dawn.
First light, soft glimmering my eyes
The sky, your arms
Wrapped in, folded closely about shimmering
Circumference of earth.
Listen
To the song of night's receding—
The long low murmur of the distancing stars,
The shuddering river,
How she carries her burdens silently
Through all the long night, then
Howls, just once before dawn.
Turning again, to receive more, receive day.
Birth, breath, burden.
Now light, new day.

Establishing a Daily Practice (and How to Keep it Going)

by Nikolai

Abstract

This little article is for you, if you are about to start any kind of daily practice, or if you have already started one and are experiencing difficulties in keeping it going.

This is not about the contents of your practice or what exercises to choose.

This can be about any kind of practice you do with the goal to grow yourself in some aspect: spiritual exercises, meditation, learning a musical instrument, dance training, martial arts, or learning to ride a unicycle.

The following reflects my experience. Some things may work differently for you. Only you can decide what is helpful to you or not.

Daily Practice as Growth

A daily practice is a growth process. This is not meant metaphorically, but literally. Even if it is not a sports activity, we change our physical body through daily practice. We build muscle. In our brain, we grow new synapses between neurons. The body alters the quantity of hormones put out at specific occasions. Our etheric body—if this concept is part of your view—changes its shape. We establish new habits.

Growth processes are usually slow. This means it is easy to assume that there is, seemingly, no effect. It is difficult to get fast feedback about whether or not we are still on track.

Many of us are more used to a short-term, cause-and-effect-paradigm of acting. I prepare a meal, and after 20 minutes it is ready to be eaten. I turn a key, then I can open the door. I drive to work, and then I have arrived.

We don't usually perform growth processes, but sometimes we take part in them—for example, when caring for a garden or raising a child. The difference with daily practice is that here we grow ourselves; we are both the caregiver and the growing being.

So let's look at some specific aspects of this self-growth process: establishing a daily practice.

Motivation

As growth is a long-term project, it is good to prepare oneself to spend at least a year with any practice leading to growth. Committing so much time to a new practice requires sound motivation.

What is your motivation?

To help clarify this, here are some questions you can ask yourself:

- What do I want to achieve with the daily practice?
- Is my goal the final goal, or is it rather a means for another goal beyond?
- If it is a means for something else, are there alternative ways to get to that "something else"?
- If it is a goal in its own right, or a necessary step to another goal, do I really want this goal?
- How might I be, what might my life look like, when I have reached that goal? How could reaching that goal affect my relations, my family, my professional life, my health, and my happiness?
- Do I really want to be like that? Do I want my life to look like that?

When asking those questions, look not only at your thoughts, but also at emotions, gut feelings, and maybe reflect on the experiences of people you know personally who have done something similar.

If these questions—and possibly others—lead to the conclusion that you really do want to start this practice, then you can look at some practical aspects.

Rhythm and Protection

Living beings love rhythm. From a good groove to the turning of day and night, taking action with rhythm makes it easier. So it is helpful to set a specific time of the day and a specific location where you want to do your practice, and do it each time at this same hour and place.

For many people it is easiest to practice just after rising in the morning, but it could be another specific time of the day, like just before dinner, or after the children are in bed.

Look at your personal daily biorhythm: Many people are especially tired after lunch. While a physical practice can wake you up then, something like meditation is better done at a time of the day when you are more awake.

If possible, choose a location where you love to be. Tell everybody you must not be disturbed. Turn off your cell phone and set the landline ringer volume to low. Shut the door if necessary. Create a space and a time that belongs solely to yourself.

If your family is not used to you being unavailable, explain to them that everybody needs a time solely for themselves—a time to refresh and "reset." Explain that you want to do something that is important for you and that it will not work if you are disturbed. They might like to discuss the fact that they themselves would like to have such a private, undisturbed time as well. You can discuss together how to make sure you can both get the time you need.

Get creative if necessary. Eileen Caddy, co-founder of the Findhorn Community, once lived with three adults and three children in one caravan. To get her daily undisturbed meditation time, she chose the loo-hut and went there in the early morning, before the rest of the family was awake. I hope, however, there will be a more convenient time and location for you.

Timing

Start as soon as possible.

If you wait for a specific meaningful date, the specificity of this date will support you in the beginning. But that support lessens quickly, and afterwards staying with your practice becomes more difficult. As a daily practice is a long—quite long—term engagement, it can be started any day. It does not matter which day.

Start short, but do it daily. Here we come to the specifics of a growth process: growth needs a daily trigger. This trigger can be brief, but it will be effective if done daily. Here comes the most important piece of this article.

If you act according to this "rule," you can forget everything else:

> *The difference in effect between practicing*
> *two minutes today versus one is 2 to 1.*
> *The difference between practicing one minute today*
> *or not at all is like 1,000,000 to 1.*

If you do one minute of real, concentrated practice each day—not lighting the candle for meditation, or slipping into the shoes for running, but the real work—then you will have some success. Practicing only once per month, even if for 6 hours, has no lasting effect at all.

This rule also applies to increasing time. Increase how often you practice before increasing how much. Should you choose to increase your practice time, for example from 6 minutes to 20, and find that 20 minutes is just not possible on a particular day, be certain to do at least 6 minutes, or even 1, rather than nothing.

Life is rarely ideal, and there have been many days when I did not manage to do my 1 minute. This may happen to you as well. So how many times a week is frequently enough?

- 3 times, well spread over the week:

In my experience, this is the minimum useful amount.

- 5 to 6 times a week:

That is good. With this frequency I can watch changes happen and feel in the flow of the process.

- 7 times a week:

While this seems the most effective, there is true wisdom in having one free day in the week. Having a short pause provides some relaxation, which stimulates growth. In my ideal practice, I take 1 or 2 days off each month.

These numbers may not apply to every practice! For example, some sports activities must not be done so often, because the body needs regeneration time—refer to your teacher or trainer.

Expectation

For many practitioners I know, the biggest trap is expectation. One would think doing anything one minute a day should be easy.

It is not.

Do not expect your daily practice to be hard to keep. But if it is, do not be surprised, and don't blame yourself. You are in good company with thousands of other humans who experience the same difficulty. Some support may be needed to do such a seemingly (but not really) simple task.

Talking Self and Instinctive Self

Originating from Huna is a concept of every human being having three "souls" or "selves":

- Our everyday consciousness that thinks, feels, communicates, explores and decides. I call this one the "Talking Self."
- The instinctive soul that controls all body functions, contains all memories, seeks to find pleasure and avoid pain, likes to play, creates emotions, contains our inner child, speaks to us in dreams and gives us the energy for living. I call this one the "Instinctive Self."
- And the divine spark, the mystery that connects each human to that what is holy to her or him, but is also a part of ourselves. I like to call it "Aumakua," its Hawaiian name.

This three selves concept is not a truth to believe, but a map of the human soul that has been useful to me. Other maps can be just as useful, but I will be using this one for the purpose of this article.

A function of Talking Self is to decide. Probably, it was your Talking Self that decided you want to start a daily practice.

A function of Instinctive Self is to provide energy. You need the consent and support of your Instinctive Self, if the daily practice is going to be a success. Instinctive Self usually likes most things that a child likes: happiness, fun, play, and rewards. It avoids anything that looks like pain, fear, disappointment.

If your Instinctive Self supports you, practicing will usually be easy. Most of the time you will enjoy your practice and spend more time with it. If your Instinctive Self does not support you, keeping the practice going will be quite a struggle.

Although Talking Self knows the good results it hopes to achieve with practice, for Instinctive Self those results are far away and unreal. In order to love daily practice and support you in doing it, Instinctive Self needs incentives, and they need to be short-term.

So what can you do to convince Instinctive Self that your daily practice is a favourable thing?

Talk with It

You can talk to your Instinctive Self in the way you might talk to a child. Many people give their Instinctive Self a name. Max F. Long, the introducer of this technique to modern Western culture, called his Instinctive Self "George."

Explain what you intend to do, why you think it is important to you, and how you want Instinctive Self to support you. Be clear and specific in what you want from it; for example: "Dear {name for your Instinctive Self}, I want to be joyful when I start my daily practice, and I want a sense of expectancy. I want to feel as though something is missing when I haven't yet done it during a day." Of course, your specific wishes can be different. Creating a positive atmosphere can be good, such as "I am really looking forward to us doing this together, and thank you very much for your support!"

When you make your explanation, remember that what Instinctive Self will understand are the emotions you radiate: if you are enthusiastic, very serious, adventurous, or hopeful, these emotions will be understandable and convincing to Instinctive Self. Factual reasoning will not be as persuasive.

Make Practicing Beautiful or Enjoyable

Associate practice with things that your Instinctive Self loves. Hang a beautiful picture at the place where you practice. Dress in some favorite clothing. Use fancy tools. Anything like that.

Adapting the Exercise Programs

Perhaps you can add an exercise that is not really necessary, but that Instinctive Self especially loves, such as at the end of your daily practice time. Or maybe you can change the direction you face, so you can look at trees or flowers instead of watching a wall.

Do not leave out exercises, however, simply because Instinctive Self does not like them. Resistance often arises at a point where growth is about to happen.

On the other hand, there do exist valid reasons to not do an exercise: your body may be harmed if it is not prepared well enough. Or your ethics may be touched. Do not do what your whole being rejects.

Be Simple

Do not start your practice with a big, fancy program with 83 details to remember that requires 2 hours 40 minutes. Start with one or very few elements. This makes it easier for Instinctive Self to adapt to the new habit. Your physical and non-physical bodies will also get a clearer message as to where growth will happen. Concentration is powerful.

The same rule applies to when you expand your practice. One day you indeed might be aware of 83 different details in your daily routine, but add them slowly.

Use the Magic of 3

All magical work—and growing and changing yourself is magic, even if your practice has no metaphysical content—benefits by the number 3. Three repetitions make a solid impression. Doing exactly three different items in a group of actions gives it momentum that can carry you, like a waltz carries you across the dance floor.

Your practice can benefit by starting with doing either one element or three. If your practice already contains more elements, you might identify groups of three items belonging together. Where repetitions occur, consider three of them.

Short-Term Rewards

Doing something that Instinctive Self really likes after you have finished your daily practice can increase its support of your work.

Visualize and Remember Long-Term Rewards Often

Expected long-term results become more real for Instinctive Self if you visualize them often, think about how you would enjoy them, and imagine how they would feel.

This is also true of positive effects of your practice that you have already noticed. Celebrate these effects, remember them regularly, and frequently and consciously recall the positive feelings you have about them.

Create a Habit

Instinctive Self loves habits, routines, and repeating rituals. If you manage to make your daily practice a habit, Instinctive Self is more likely to support it.

Some sources say that doing a thing 21 days without interruption creates a habit. Other sources claim 36 days are necessary. I have found that even 36 days are not enough in some cases. Once, my Instinctive Self was very happy we had reached this result and went off to relax… forget about establishing that "habit."

Nevertheless, practicing for 21 or 36 days without interruption can be helpful. This guideline is supposed to help you, not deflate you. If it does not work, you can use some of the other techniques described here.

Find Co-Practitioners

One of the most supportive things you can do is to find co-practitioners who face similar challenges and exchange experiences with them regularly. This does not require people who do the same practice as you. If you find others who want to start a practice they need to do daily, that may be already enough commonality for a fruitful exchange.

Missing Days, Weeks, Months

You can start every day. And, you can re-start every day. If you have lost your practice routine, do not despair, do not blame yourself, do not think anything is lost. Certainly do not think that everything is lost.

Just start again. One minute a day. Have fun!

You can always do this, even after a pause of 6 months. You can go now, practice a short time, and you are back on your way.

If you have missed some time, be gentle with yourself, because Instinctive Self hates pain, disappointment and bad temper. Be friendly to yourself, and start again.

You may find it helpful to talk to Instinctive Self and ask: What is it that bothers or hinders you? Is there anything that needs to change? Be clear, however, that you will continue, and that you still wish to have Instinctive Self's support.

If practice does not run as you intended, do not forget humor. Being able to smile about one's own little mishaps and imperfections is one of the most powerful healing methods.

Conclusion

Establishing a daily practice is similar to tending a growing plant. Daily care is needed, but one does not see immediate results. Daily practice is a co-creation of yourself, of all the parts within you, and the powers of nature and of spirit. It benefits from love, patience and curiosity.

Like tending plants, daily practice is an opportunity to trigger and watch growth, actively participating in one of the great mysteries of nature. Unlike tending plants, you can watch the growth and experience it from inside. You are the plant and the tender of the plant, all at once.

I wish you joy and success with your practice and the growth for which you are aiming.

Gratitude:
A Meditation and Paean

by Kevin Faulkner

We give witness
To the beautiful world around us.
We relax our bodies
Air flows in
We contract
Air flows out.
The sun shines
Warming life upon the brow;
We know gratitude.
Clouds wash with cleansing rain and cooling shade;
We give thanks.
The Mother makes of herself
Leaf and fruit and seed

Fliers crawlers swimmers and walkers
We eat Her.
We are Her.
We are grateful.

Gratitude serves as a powerful form of manifestation magic, and it is the magic of gratitude that enables us to keep in our lives that which we value. That for which we do not cultivate appreciation may be neglected and break or leave our lives. Our attention to the history of things also reminds us that all that has form in this world is ephemeral, a momentary configuration of consciousness, matter, information, energy, spirit. When something or someone inevitably leaves our lives, the pain is heightened by an awareness of our own ingratitude; by definition, we failed to appreciate what we had while we had it. Though the suffering may still be great when something or someone for which or whom we have been grateful leaves or dies, we have the comfort of knowing we strove for full presence and appreciation while we sojourned together. The bitter waters of parting may be made more palatable for us if we save ourselves from the draught of regret as well.

When we eat food that was tortured, or processed in Earth-torturous ways, gratitude practice can return us to mindfulness of that fact. It is easier to give thanks and rejoice in a life well lived in sunshine, health, and freedom and sacrificed for our well-being. Awareness enhances our desire to eat food that was itself properly treated, properly fed. When we give thanks for the beings and existences around us, when we give honor and reverence to their value, we see how they benefit us and the entire web of life. We may begin to imagine more vividly and honestly how we also benefit the web around us, and come to value ourselves more highly. As we develop the true desire to nurture ourselves better as an essential part of our responsibility to the whole, that desire transfers sincerely to the beings who nourish us. When we have to remind ourselves of the tremendous and unnecessary suffering generated by an industrialized food system, we may feel guilt, or pain. We can transform that pain into conviction and commitment to work for a more just world, for a more just, healthy, and sustainable food system. When I buy food for my own home, I refuse to buy anything but the most pampered meat, even if that means I am more "moderate" in my meat consumption than I might otherwise be. But when someone extends to me the hospitality of whatever they can and choose to afford, I would be ashamed to scorn their gift. This magic of gratitude and re-commitment helps to transmute my food, my relationship to it, and my sacred body, without scorning holy hospitality.

These same truths apply across the board. Gratitude is clearly no scarcity mentality, but neither is it a naïve specter of abundance thinking. It is harder to move into a rigidly individualistic possessiveness with our belongings when we recognize how they came to us, but we also appreciate more deeply what we have. Without gratitude we become readier prey to many vices: holy pride and desire married to ingratitude become an ossified entitlement and a bottomless greed. Pride and gratitude, however, show us as an essential and beautiful face of the Goddess, capable of giving as we ourselves are given to. The cultural spell of individualism and consumerism is unmade by the deeper and more beautiful magics of graciousness and interdependence, and we are attuned to the joy of the constant flow of life around us.

Gratitude embeds us more deeply into the cosmic dance of giving. Knowing the universe to be a giving place, it is easier to place ourselves into a place where we can receive what we need and desire. To put it another way, as we create a dynamic of gratitude, giving and generosity, we resonate micro-to macrocosmically with the universe and open the roads by which magic may assist us in fulfilling our needs, enhancing our capacity for manifestation. Gratitude also provides a balance so that our capacity for magic doesn't become a sort of spiritualized consumerism. New Thought ("you create your own reality") is experiencing a rebirth through the vehicle of *The Secret* and *The Law of Attraction*. Many people attempt to apply this solipsistic perspective to their lives with a kind of cosmic shopping-mall mentality and, taken literally, this kind of thinking slides almost instantly into a kind of unconscionable victim blaming.

By acknowledging relationship and fostering a vision of embeddedness in the endlessly transforming song of life, we remind ourselves that, in fact, all beings are constantly co-creating this life. Sometimes unthinkable things happen to us because of the decisions of other actors around us who do not foster deep connection and guidance with the sources of wisdom and life. Sometimes a Titan shifts in her sleep and a volcano or tsunami consumes a city. It is nothing personal; it is merely a difference in scale, just as we may unknowingly crush a small bug underfoot unawares or catch a beautiful butterfly in our wheel as we move about in our efforts to live our lives and better the world. New Thought philosophies are often appealing to those who enjoy financial, racial, or other privilege, and most of whose problems really do exist in their minds. Of course, our minds are as real as the rest of the universe. And, when we begin to sit in meditation with our minds, we may see that although we may be *able* to create the realities inside our heads, our mind typically goes along creating itself just like the rest of the cosmos and that creating our own reality even there may require a surprising amount of work!

Practicing gratitude, then, as a window to connection, we recognize that things may happen to people that are beyond their power, but we may also begin to see our own roles in the larger patterns around us. Poverty in the colonized world is not due to the improper thinking of the impoverished, but rather due to the systems that systematically steal from and disenfranchise them as they privilege and enrich the first world, particularly its most affluent members. As we become more aware of this, again, we may also become more critical of our use of the word "need," and whether we need something in our life at all, much less whether we need to use magic to call it to us from beyond our present reach! As we are more grateful for and knowledgeable about the beautiful Earth-system of which we are an incarnate piece, we may wonder whether we "need" some new toy or luxury food that can only exist or come to us after a process of violent extraction from the body of the Earth and violent exploitation in labor practices. We can waste less of our lives and magical effort on that which we do not need, and free ourselves up for greater joy and service.

This is not the same as sliding into puritanical patterns of self-denial. Negative morality, fixated on avoiding doing "bad" things, is of no interest to me. My practice of gratitude and the sense of mutual responsibility it engenders in me does not allow me simply to avoid doing harm;

it calls me instead to make the most good I am able. If I truly do need something to live my life and pursue the Work of this God, or my True Will, and I am only able to obtain it through the economy of extraction and exploitation, just as with food, I strive to transmute my complicity in the process to a commitment to justice and change. All things are part of this world and this human experience belongs to us all; I attempt to refuse the heady intoxicant of self-righteousness and remind myself that we are all in it together and none of us is above it.

Let us be grateful for the goodness we have, for the goodness we know, and for the goodness we are. We give thanks for our blessedness. May we share our goodness and blessedness for the blessing and highest good of all beings in every time and world.

O, Death—
Meditations on
Life's Impermanence

by Rynn Fox

The Sweet and the Sting

What makes life sweet, wild and precious? Perhaps the scent of jasmine on the night air, a scrap of food in a hungry tummy, the bonds of familial kinship, a smile from a random stranger, camaraderie, sweat-slicked skin from lovemaking, or the relief of feeling healthy again. Life brings us responsibilities, realities, and trials that oftentimes weigh heavily on our minds, bodies, emotions and spiritual selves. In our rush to survive, and hopefully thrive, it's easy to forget the sweetness and simple pleasure of living, of being. Yet in order to savor the sweet, we must acknowledge and accept the sting.

You are going to die. It will not be at a time of your choosing, most likely.

Yet this fact does not have to be bitter or frightening. Death and the impermanent fluidity of life are gifts; a natural counterpoint to life. Just as music is the arrangement of sound and silence, so is Death the silence to life's wall of sound. Fear of Death, of change, and impermanence shackles us with deep-seated fears of the unknown and of the loss of predictability that life brings us. Life and living are the only things we have ever known and experienced. To us, Death is a vast nothingness where we have no experience to root our ideas in. Thus our fears are triggered. It is our lack of familiarity with Death that compounds these very human, very real fears to the point of avoidance.

This is where the value of Death meditations enters. When we face and accept impermanence and Death, life opens up for us. Time has the opportunity to slow. Yes, time still rushes like sand through a sieve, but our perception of it is altered. We are better equipped to notice and enjoy each precious grain of sand before it slips through the sieve into the firmament. We do not grasp and instead choose to enjoy each moment in its time and reflection. Our experience of time lengthens when we allow ourselves to fully hold both life and Death in our awareness. After a time of practice, we are able to stand between these two poles and experience with rapt attention the awesome and inspiring tension of the retreating middle ground that lies between them. In that lengthening of time and widening of awareness, the full weight of each individual moment, as well as the spectrum of human experience—our emotions, thoughts, choices, tastes, smells, and sounds—are experienced fully, viscerally. The shackles are broken in accepting Death. Life is revealed as a heady, sensual banquet offering a rich experience of joy and sweet suffering, aching love and bitter irony, moments of selflessness and selfishness, desire, lust, complication and simplicity, rage, fierce compassion and more, so much more.

Exercise One—From Death, Life

Stop. Take in a breath and follow it down, down into your lungs. Feel your lungs expand and the air move into the tiny branches of your capillaries, the thicker veins. Breathe again and follow it down, down, down into your lungs. Feel the air electric and moving fast, a torrential current of life force as it moves on a journey with a singular purpose: to keep life in the brain. Feel the torrent stop; the life giving air flows no further, instead decaying. A mad, fumbling panic explodes in your body briefly, only to succumb to an expanding feeling of weakness, of ground lost, or receding, falling away, or powerlessness…and futility. Then a feeling of dissolving; light dims the groundlessness as the feeling of dissolving grows, expands one last time, then…nothing. You float, and yet you feel nothing. You know nothing. But something is capable of noticing that the unmaking has begun. You feel your blood, once the carrier of oxygen and life, turn acidic...and begin to burn, bearing down on each cell in your body... Feel each cell as it bursts, flooding your body with more enzymes that devour and soften... You begin to melt: your muscle, ligaments, bones, and organs. Your organs begin to digest themselves, disintegrating into residue. And yet you feel life—powerful, and thrumming with vivacious abundance as the billions of one-celled organisms, once held in check by symbiosis, now burst forth like a horde to feast, devouring your guts. And you notice the sweet water, the liquid that helped power your actions, settle amongst the iron of your blood and pass down through the dissolving mire that was once your body to touch the dirt beneath you. You notice the Earth beneath you, how it rises up to cradle your dwindling form, accepting, absorbing, and receiving you back into Her body... The carrion eaters—winged, crawling, and four-legged—rip, tear, and devour you, fueling their own life with your flesh... And you expand out, flooding the body of the Earth with what little is left of your flesh until only the bones remain...as the weather and the movement of seasons do their part as well... The Sun, so hot and harsh, bakes your bones into brittleness...followed by the chill of autumn and winter's icy grip snapping bones into fragments upon fragments... Then the first of spring's zephyrs stirs your icy grave and again you feel life, pushing up from the ground beneath you... New shoots of life fertilized by your Death push up through the soil, through the last remnants of your body; fueled by your Death, they now rise with life.

Pause for a moment in the silence of new life out of Death. Let yourself open to the wisdom of the moment. Let any additional information come into you. When you feel ready, focus your attention upon your breath. With every inhalation, widen your attention further. Feel your lungs expand within you and your shoulders rise. Feel the breath move deep into your diaphragm and shoulders, arms and thighs, neck and legs. Lastly, send a breath to your crown and feet. Open your eyes. Feel yourself back fully within your body.

Life, Death, and Impermanence

Death is a process a lifetime in the making. That process looks like aging. From the moment we are born, we are dying. Even as we live, Death is with us in every life change and transition. On the day of our birth, Death is there, pushing us out of the relative safety of mother's womb into a frighteningly bright world and unfamiliar hands; when a childhood best friend moves away, never to be heard from again; when we enter a relationship, and again when the relationship ends; in our bodies as we age from infant to child, adolescent to adult, and (hopefully) senior citizen. Death is the locus of these moments, softly whispering to us that every moment changes and that every facet of life is impermanent. These changes are felt and seen the most viscerally in the vehicle of aging, where they manifest. True, the changes are subtle at first—the loss of baby teeth, the growth from adolescent to adult—but they soon give way to rapid and often unwelcome changes: wrinkles, hair loss, reduced physical ability, and more. These changes seem to steal our very sense of self, but a self based on physical capability. Through aging, we are able to both witness and experience the evidence of our own impermanent nature. Time marches across our bodies, leaving telltale signs warning us that with each passing second, we are being brought closer to our inevitable final destination: Death.

Exercise Two—Aging and the Soul

Items needed: One mirror that can reflect your entire face at minimum.

Before beginning this meditation, please take a few moments to search your psyche, soul, and body for awareness of your spirit's energy signatures: the almighty I AM. When "found," this signature is markedly different from your body's and psyche's energy signatures. Energy quality and resonance mark the difference between them. You will need to discover for yourself what markers denote which energy signature is which.

In a darkened room, place the mirror in front of you. Level of light should be such that your face is barely visible in the mirror. Sit or stand comfortably. Close your eyes. Begin to breathe deeply. As you exhale, let your muscles soften and relax; all tension melts away. Continue to breathe deeply. Imagine there is a pool of calm nested within the space just behind your navel. Breathe deeply into that place of serenity, allowing a sense of ease to fill you. Continue to breathe deeply and sink into the feeling of ease arising from the pool.

O, DEATH

If stray thoughts arise, let them pass by like a leaf on a stream and return to the pool. Feel yourself sinking deeper and deeper until you have a sense of arriving at the bottom of this pool. Here tranquility enrobes you entirely with comfort. Rest here for a moment or two. When you feel ready, form the intention to know and feel your soul's energy signature. If a phrase would help, say "I am open to my soul's energy, let me know my sense of I AM." Gently hold this intention in your mind. If this thought were a ball, you would hold it cupped loosely in your open palm. If this image helps you focus your intention, use it. Let this intention grow stronger with certainty and focus. When the intention feels complete, release it into the pool. Settle back into the feeling of calm and ease. Continue to breathe deeply.

Open your field of awareness. Imagine fingers of energy moving into the pool, following your intention down, down, down…to land at the bottom of the pool…to touch an energetic pearl, pulsing with life…pulsing with a sense that can only be described as I AM. Immerse your entire awareness in this sense, this I AM, that is untouched by age, form, or circumstance. Note your impressions about this energetic impression of your soul. It may come across as an energetic quality, or perhaps a color, a collection of sounds or one lone tone, a resonance, or some other impression. Immerse yourself in this energy. Bathe every sense in it. When you are full of your I AM, begin to remember how you felt five years ago. Feel the quality vitality your body had then in your bones and flesh. Remember how your mind felt. Remember how your soul felt. Notice how and where these qualities are different and same. Take whatever time you need to fully experience being five years younger. When you feel ready, open your eyes and look into mirror. See yourself as you were five years prior. Perhaps there are fewer wrinkles, or your hairstyle has changed. As you envision this, continue to breathe in this sense of I AM, begin to shift your focus to your body. Touch your face in the mirror. Let your awareness feel your body's signature. Notice where or if it aligns with your I AM and or where it is different. Repeat this process again, going ten years back. Then when you feel ready, remember yourself as you are now. Breathe deeply into your body and allow yourself to experience it fully. See your current self in the mirror and continue to hold a light awareness of your soul's signature apart from your body's resonance. Now we will move forward in time. Deepen your awareness of your soul signature and begin to envision your face and body aging. See the lines on your face build in prominence. Age spots on your neck and hands appear and darken. Feel vitality and flexibility go out of your body; your flesh begin to sag with the weight of time. Your finger joints stiffen with age, making movement more difficult and painful. Your gums become tender with the ache of age. Sounds are muted more and more as your hearing decreases. See yourself fully as an aged human…and notice that you are still you. Your body has changed; your soul and personality have not.

When you feel ready, close your eyes and once again drop your awareness to your belly and breathe deep. Remember yourself as you are now. Savor the feel of ability and vitality in your body as it is now and give thanks. Touch your hands to your legs, arms, shoulders, face, and lastly, heart, as you give honor to yourself for this new awareness.

Legacy

What is legacy? We are the inheritors of a multitude of legacies going back a few decades, and a hundred thousand years. From ideas to societal "norms," each generation has left its indelible impression on the world and our lives. These legacies are definitely a mixed bag. So too will ours be. But in acknowledging the power we have in the present as living beings, we are able to better shape what endowments we leave to the world.

You have been sowing the seeds of your legacy since the day you were born. With every thought, word, non-action, and deed you have marked the world and humankind. You will continue to leave your personal stamp on every moment of every day until you die. What do you imagine your legacy is currently?

Many people think of legacy in terms of large acts and sweeping gestures, but small acts of respect, kindness, and generosity amount to large acts over a lifetime. How would people remember you if you died right now? What endowments have you passed on to your loved ones? How about the surly teenager working at the drug store? Have you bestowed the world with gifts of kindness, fierce compassion, and love, or hurt and unseemly habits?

A little bit of both, or perhaps too much of one and not the other? Have your habits or traditions brought people together or divided them? What small acts of kindness and love have you sown in the wider world? Perhaps your act of goodwill was paying for a stranger's groceries in the market or the easy kindness of a smile and small talk to a homeless person down on their luck. What slights—both unintentional and intentional—have borne poison fruit?

Is your legacy all that you want it to be?

Exercise Three—Momento Mori

Find a place to lie comfortably. Loosen any clothing that may irritate you. Close your eyes and breathe deep into your solar plexus. Let any tension in your muscles relax and soften. Imagine any stray thoughts evaporating with each breath. Again breathe into the well of calmness behind your navel. Feel the energy inherent in each breath and let it feed the well until a feeling of calm purpose spills forth from the well of your navel. Feel this sense of calm life force fill you to the brim. Push the energy into the aura surrounding your body, flaring your energy body wider. Feel your astral body begin to lift out of your physical body; rising higher and higher. Envision yourself moving through the ceiling, out of the house, and into the sky. You fly higher and higher past the clouds, through the ozone layer and into the solar system. Ahead you notice an area of star-studded sky, murky and grey. You begin to fly towards it, into it. A low hum of energy surrounds you, carrying you forward of its own volition.

O, Death

Pulling you towards a blinding light that is moving closer, and closer, and closer until it swallows your entire vision...and delivers you to a room. This room is unknown to you. But the people within it: you know many of them. The identities of others are a mystery. You can see they are sad. You notice them gathered around something and move to see it. It is a photo memorial of you. You look again at the faces of those gathered and both family and friends weeping. One moves forward to press a hand to the picture frame. You have the sense that they are wishing for one last time to say the words that went unsaid. You overhear a snippet of conversation. "I wished I'd been a priority. I wish I had more happy memories. But that hope has died now, hasn't it?" You see your beloved standing quietly, a look of agony on their tear-streaked face. You notice someone else in the midst of this crowd of mourners roll their eyes and check the time. Their thought comes to you: "Good riddance."

As you look over the mourners gathered in your memory, ask yourself: "What has my legacy been to these people?" As you look at each person individually, ask yourself, "What has been my legacy to you?" Let the answer fill your awareness with each person you ask. After you have gathered the awareness of the very last person, you feel the low hum returning to air. The room begins to fade to white light. Again you are flying downward into the star field. Then the Earth's atmosphere. The light recedes behind you. You move down through the clouds until you see a familiar roof. You fly through it easily and come to your body, lying where you left it. You place your astral hands on your physical hands. The sensation of being gently and easily pulled into your body envelops you. Feel your astral body fill your feet, your calves…then your thighs and sex. Your soul fills your torso, shoulders, arms and hands…welling up into your neck, face, ears, forehead, and lastly, the crown of your head.

Breathe deeply and open your awareness to the feeling of your lungs expanding and contracting with each breath. Wiggle your fingers and toes. When you feel ready, open your eyes and rise. Ground and center. If need be, eat some protein and carbohydrates to further ground you.

What Do You Live For?

Fear of Death is fear of the unknown. It's the same fear that keeps us holding on to something that is past its prime, its usefulness. It keeps us from making a necessary change because we can't know the repercussions. We have only the experience of being alive. Death is the thing we don't know. Few have returned with a firsthand account, and it's easy for many people to discount those accounts for whatever reason. Our natural human fear of the unknown, and of Death, is compounded by our lack of familiarity with Death.

For many people living in first world countries, accepting Death is either a horrible idea to avoid at all costs, or an intellectual exercise that never quite makes it past Ego's filter to percolate in the deep chasms of our awareness where it can take root. Why waste time on unpleasant thoughts? Better to sweep them under the proverbial rug.

Both as individuals and as a society we are divorced from witnessing the very human process of dying and the experience of Death. For those of us in the Western world, society further aids and abets us by intentionally blinding us from this reality. It was the family's responsibility to tend to the dying and bury the dead little more than a hundred years ago. Now it's left to the "experts" so that our loved ones undergoing the journey of dying can be "better taken care of." We are even insulated from witnessing and participating in the slaughter of the animals whose roasted, freeze-dried, or fried flesh fill our bellies to fullness night after night.

As Death is difficult to find in our sequestered modern lives, we must visit Her.

Some traditions hold that going to the realm of the Dead is folly. Others say that meeting Death is a sure way to become dead faster. This is not true. Death serves life. Yes, She feeds off life, but that is nature's way. In turn, the living takes sustenance from the dead. Something must die for the living to live. Life in turn needs Death to clear the way. It is a symbiotic, cyclic relationship. By meeting Death first hand, we are often able to have a better glimpse of our place in life. And learn deeper lessons regarding why we fear Death.

Exercise Four—Visiting Death

Lie comfortably in a dim room where you will not be disturbed. Make sure that you are fully comfortable. Close your eyes. Breathe deep. Imagine a deep feeling of calm entering you as you inhale. Feel this bone-deep sense of calm spill out of your pores with every exhalation. Notice where there is tension within your body. Send a breath of ease there. Let the tension melt, then turn into relaxation. Continue breathing deep, deeper, deeper...until you feel your body begin to sink down. You are moving downward through a tunnel in the Earth. The smell of wet dirt is thick in your nostrils. See the soil, the bits of root sticking from the tunnel walls. The light from your room is softening and dimming as you descend further down...down...down. The light from above disappears and yet the air shimmers with soft, blue glow. You are now stand at the mouth of a cave looking out into a landscape bleached of color. A haze of white-gold light illuminates the landscape. Pause. Notice your surroundings. As you take in the view, you feel a prickle run up your spine. You know you are not alone. You notice the haze has become thicker to your right...and it's moving toward you rapidly. It engulfs you. There is nothing but the swirl of haze around you... Then you notice movement. A figure in white moves toward you. Their hood is up, masking their face. They are holding something. But what? Closer, closer, closer the figure comes until you can see what they are holding: a scythe. The figure raises its face to look at you. A woman's face looks back: blue translucent skin covers a skeletal figure. You can see the ghost of the person that was and bones underneath. You look into the eyes of Death. She holds Her hand out to you. Your heart begins to pound in fright. "I did not offer you my scythe," She says. "You seek answers, yes? Let us walk together. You ask. I may answer." You take Death's hand and begin to walk beside Her.

Take as long as you need with Her. When you feel ready to depart, ask Death to lead you back to the cave. Thank Her for the journey. If She will not, just thinking about it will call you back there. Feel yourself again rise up through the tunnel in the Earth…rising higher and higher. The smell of loam again fills your nostrils. The pitch black fades to a soft light, then a warmer light. You rise higher and higher until you again are in your room. Breathe deeply. Feel vitality filling you with every inhalation and fueling you with every exhalation. Continue to breathe until you feel ready to open your eyes. Ensure you are fully back in your body before continuing with your day. Remember to ground, center, and have a little protein to get you fully present in the here and now.

Testament—A Prayer

The lessons Death brings to us continually evolve. The teaching brought to us at thirteen will bear different fruit when re-encountered at thirty-three. It's for this reason that a prayer to Death is part of my daily practice. I recite this prayer as I eat a teaspoon of honey. For me, the honey represents the sweetness of life.

May this prayer, and these workings, help you live a good life.

And a good death.

Lady Death,
In this melody of life I move to,
Help me hear your counterpoint,
So that when I move,
Whether with poise or wild abandon
Under the hot sun or withering rain
I fully dance the gift of life as entrusted to me

Lady Death,
Shine the light of living for me
Help me make my life wild and holy,
Precious and sweet,
Whether confronted with
Beauty or terror, hurt or amazement

Lady Death,
Help me make my life
True and honest and honorable
Or rather the result of all of things combined:
Grace-filled, graceful, and beautiful.

Entering the Temple of the Morningstar: For Those Who Fear "Astral Rejection"

by Fortuna

I distinctly remember my response to Thorn's announcement that advanced students of Morningstar Mystery School would be meeting each New Moon to work in an Astral Temple.

"It's bollocks," announced my Talker. "Come on. Really?"

Fetch felt a lot of resistance, too. We had tried, although in hindsight not hard enough, to do astral projection a few times in life. It hadn't deployed. Fetch hates failure. We were scared.

Still—all the other Morningstar kids seemed really keen. They seemed to think the idea of a group Astral Temple was cool. So there it was. Peer pressure. The need to perform had most certainly gotten me to at least *try* to believe things my Talker was ready to dismiss without a second thought earlier in my training.

So, with a printout of the procedure for reaching the Temple clutched to my none-too-confident bosom, I figured "what the heck" and made my first attempt to get to the shared place-that-is-not-a-place. I aligned, lit my Star Goddess candle while saying the Holy Mother prayer, made kala, and got ready for what I hoped would be a vivid experience.

Is It Just a "Castle in the Air"?

Working in an Astral Temple can, like much astral work, seem nebulous to we embodied humans. The idea of our New Moon visit is wonderfully like something in Young Adult fiction. We travel from physical locations all over the world. We seek knowledge that has been "seeded" by the architects of the Temple. We enrich and re-create the school egregore each time we show up for a visit.

Work in the Astral Temple can be beautiful; it can be confusing; it can be daunting. It can be profound, too. And I want to tell you, reader: you might just doze off during a visit.

One Temple Fits All. It Can Just Look and Feel Really Different for Everyone

One of the curious qualities of group work on the astral is that, although certain architectural features tend to remain constant for all members of the group, the form of the Temple is prone to sudden changes and "renovations" we don't expect or understand. Often this is the result of our personal overlays—the allies, Gods, practices, aesthetics, history, memories, and needs we bring to this work—which make the "flavor" of the Temple different for each of us. Our experiences may include other students, who are sometimes surprised to hear about being "seen" by others. Sometimes, it's even difficult to get through the front door. I had problems for months when I was studying concurrently with another teacher in a different line. I had no idea why I couldn't get in. My conclusion is that the Temple is warded quite effectively!

The inconsistencies of the reported group experience are what make Talker say, "Yeah. Right. Uh-huh," in that snarky way. Paradoxically, I think this is the source of a lot of the value in this work we each seem to receive the information we need in a unique manner.

Example: You have a vivid impression of a God or Goddess who "isn't supposed to be there" according to the group protocol, but who appears to you uniquely, and with whom you begin working.

Example: You have a sexually charged encounter with a divine or non-corporeal Being.

Example: The interior of the temple is completely different during one of your visits, or you discover a new "room."'

My most definitively "real" experiences in the Temple have been thoroughly my own. For example, I kept falling through the reflecting pool and coming up in another temple's pool, much like that scene in one of the *Pirates of the Caribbean* films, in which the ship flips 180 degrees and comes up in a parallel world. Eventually, another dear teacher let me know that I was entering HER temple in this way, like Alice through the looking-glass. Suddenly I understood the astral—like the "real world"—really does exist, albeit with its own rules and laws.

DIY Astral Temple?

After several years of working within the Temple at the New Moon (and sometimes at other times…it's nice and quiet!), I had the opportunity to take Thorn's workshop on building one's own astral temple.

Creating my own temple has been a real help to me, as astral work has never been the easiest thing for my ADHD-ish self to do. When I go to the Temple "cold," I have noticed that I can get distracted, or pop back into my body, or perhaps drift into sleep. Some months, making the Temple visit has taken a giant act of will, thanks to my technical difficulties on the astral.

My own temple, which is quite new and still under construction, immediately featured a "room of peace and light" through which I can very easily reach the shared Temple.

As a mystic or magic-worker, you may want to build your own temple. Please know that this personal astral temple is distinct from the "place of power" that you might have accessed through other kinds of work. And your temple will take on a life of its own. Don't be surprised to find it shifting, growing, or moving. It's like Hogwarts.

A Phased Timeline of My Own Experience

Phase One: You've got to be kidding.

Yes, my initial response to the "virtual" learning in our group's Temple was just that. Swell—more effort spent on something that I don't really think is useful, and that I'll have to check in about. And that I honestly don't believe in. (Eyes roll.)

Phase Two: Protocol and practice.

Yes, there is a protocol for getting to the Temple. Yes, getting there involves practicing this protocol once each month. The protocol has changed over time, largely under the guidance of students I barely know. The Merkabah? Bah! (Impatient sigh.) More work. Grand.

Phase Three: Am I doing this right?

Akin to chewing gum, tap dancing, and patting head while rubbing stomach all at once, there is a lot to remember and coordinate about getting to and being in the Temple, which can get in the way of the experience. (Performance anxiety. And all the other kids are having these profound experiences that they are checking in about AT LENGTH. Teeth grind.)

Phase Four: This is it!

Group check-ins about the shared Astral Temple DO indicate some crossover of experience! Hey—even though it doesn't always feel real, there is something to this! We're playing in the Mystery together! I saw A. and she saw me! There really WAS an Egyptian guardian at the door! There is a new staircase…and T. saw it too…cool!

Phase Five: Answers and depth.

The highly personal nature of work in our Astral Temple is beginning to offer extraordinarily vivid experiences that are opening me to new potentials, new voices, and providing answers to some deep-seated issues. My Gods are there, and it is easier to hear Them. Hmmm…

Phase Six: "Your actual experience may vary."

It will. Don't worry. Over time, with practice, the fluffy and elusive material of astral work begins to twist into a resilient thread thanks to our continuing attempts. Some months are vivid, deep and profound; others, you may drift off to sleep. And over time it just doesn't matter. Our threads are twining with everyone else's astral threads. Together we are weaving a tapestry of beauty and clarity.

For the Descendants

We are making and remaking, expanding and reinforcing, the Temple when we do our work as mystics in the Morningstar tradition. The Temple will be left to our descendants. So every New Moon, when I—sometimes still groaning "Do I HAVE to?" in that pubescent fashion—prepare myself and enter the Temple and ask, humbly, what has been seeded for MY healing and growth? I am not only receiving. I am sharing.

For those who struggle in earlier stages of this work—on the focus, discipline, and BELIEF it requires—I want to ask you: Have you done beautiful and "real" and significant work in trance? I would imagine so. Do visit your astral temple, over and over, with an open heart and a trust in the reality of this space. This may be the Next Big Step in your magickal evolution.

This article originally appeared in a slightly different form as a blog post on www.heartofthewitch.eu

Pagan Values

by Ealasaid A. Haas

Pagan Values Blogging Month is an annual shindig in which pagan bloggers the Web over write about Pagan Values. After a couple years of muttering "next year..." I decided to dive in! The result was a series of meandering blog posts in June 2012, all on the subject of "Pagan Values"—which I take to mean "Values Which I, A Pagan, Hold."

Firstly: "WTF do you mean by Pagan?" I hear some of you cry, and with good reason. "Pagan" is such a friggin' huge umbrella term that it's almost meaningless. Someone who is a hardcore reconstructionist trying to recreate the religion of Classical Greece is a Pagan. So is someone who wanders around in fairy wings and says "Harm None!" a lot and worships the moon.

When I say I'm a Pagan, I mean that I am a polytheist (although one who is agnostic on the "all Gods are one

God" thing) who worships multiple Gods, seeks out mystical connection with the Universe, and sees all creation as sacred. I study with Thorn Coyle, who somehow manages to be both a Pagan mystic and a skeptical academic; one of the fiercest, mostly strong-willed and disciplined people I know and also one of the kindest and most generously loving. I greatly admire that, and aspire to emulate her.

I have a lot of values—I resonate with the seven virtues of Bushido, for example, and have been very tempted to join in the long-term blogging project about the Delphic Maxims—but for now I'm going to focus on the big ones, the ones that I keep coming back to over and over, the ones that feel like mine rather than like someone else's. They are

- Experiential Pragmatism
- Integrity
- Fierce Compassion
- Love / Reverence for the Sacred
- Will / Self-Knowledge

Let's take a look at 'em a little more closely, one at a time, shall we?

Experiential Pragmatism

Back in college, I took philosophy classes. One of the things we talked about is the idea that you can't really know that anything exists, because our senses can be deceived. I could be a brain in a vat being fed information by an evil scientist, and there's no real way to know! It's the philosophical construct that brought us *The Matrix*, and just about everyone's run across it.

But here's the thing: so what? Yeah, ok, it's a mindfuck to think about that, but does it help me live my daily life?

Well, it tells me that just because I think I see something doesn't mean it's real. We've all heard about the unreliability of eyewitness testimony, so that's not exactly news—but beyond that, there's no real point to doubting my perceptions too much because they're all I have. Sure, I could be a brain in a vat, but I strongly suspect that stepping out in front of a car will still suck a whole lot. I could be a brain in a vat, but if I put bread in a toaster and toast it just right, and eat it, it's still tasty.

Until Lawrence Fishburne shows up to offer me two pills, it behooves me to act like this world is real. I don't have to know why a toaster works in order to put bread in and get toast. I don't have to know why going through a particular set of actions is generally followed by me finding a good job in order to use those actions when I'm out of work. The fact that those actions include lighting a candle and tossing coins in a fountain as well as polishing my resume and researching employers before I send it to them is irrelevant. It *works*.

I approach the gods the same way. "When I do X, Y is the result" is what matters to me. When I attend (or perform) a ritual dedicated to a deity, I have particular deity-related experiences. Those experiences enrich my life and help me solve problems. That is what matters to me, not the Grand Underlying Truth™. I don't care whether "All Gods are one God!" or "All Gods are individuals!" or "All Gods are delusions in my brain!" It'd be interesting to know, but since I *can't* know, it's irrelevant. What I care about is what I experience.

When I do magic, I get results. Is it because I'm priming myself psychologically to be alert for opportunities? Is it because I'm sending energy into the world that makes things happen? That is irrelevant. Sure, it's interesting, but given our current state of technology, it's unknowable.

If you ask me whether I believe in the Gods I worship, you might as well ask me whether I believe in rocks, or in postal workers. I don't believe. I know what I've experienced.

That is what I mean by "experiential pragmatism."

Victor Anderson, founder of the Anderson Feri Tradition and one of Thorn's teachers, used to say something along the lines of "First perceive, then believe." That's what I'm talking about. If you believe first, your perceptions can get warped. I try to set aside my expectations before ritual and just pay attention to what happens.

I place a far higher value on knowledge gained from personal experience than on knowledge gained from books—and if you know how much I love books, you know how much I value experience. My favorite Tarot card is the Hanged Man—the one who learns through action and suffering.

I learn by doing. I meet my Gods by doing. I value the concrete over the abstract. Yes, I love intellectual and theoretical discussion, but where the rubber meets the road is what matters. Talking about politics is interesting, but giving money and time to causes is what matters. Voting is what matters. I love talking about the Gods, but actually having a devotional practice is what matters.

There was an e-mail forward going around years ago that I loved, which described all the different majors in college.

The line for Philosophy was: "The class where you decide the universe does not exist, and then break for lunch."

I care about lunch.

Integrity

Thorn talks about integration and alignment a great deal, and I've picked up her emphasis on it in my years of training with her. We all have many disparate parts, and working toward becoming better and more fulfilled people means coming to know those parts and finding ways for them all to work together—finding ways to become more integrated, to have more integrity.

For me, integrity means acting from a place of integration and alignment. It means I keep my word, I speak honestly, and I strive to be truly myself everywhere, rather than being one person at work and another at home, and yet another with one friend and another with others.

It's not easy, of course. It's in our nature to have different parts, and to have different parts tend to show up in different places. It's in our nature to have emotions rise up and make us act impulsively, suddenly—and usually in ways we regret later.

Integrity means getting to know all those parts and getting them to work together rather than one lunging to take control and then another wresting control away, over and over. Integrity doesn't mean those parts all somehow fuse into one mystical Mega-Ealasaid—it means they all work together and are aimed in the same direction (which is toward my Will, but we'll get to that in a bit!).

In one of her online teaching videos, Thorn talks about the idea of a person being sort of like a horse-drawn carriage. There's the carriage (the body), horse (the emotions), driver (ego / talking mind), and the master, the one inside the carriage (our higher self / connection to the divine). All four parts have to work together to get to the master's ultimate destination—the carriage can't move without the horses, the horses won't take direction without the driver, and the driver won't know where to go without the master. Integrity is when all four pieces work together.

What's awesome is that when I'm in alignment, when I'm integrated, it helps me be consistent. It helps me to speak the hard truth instead of letting child-me take over and tell the easy white lie. It helps me to apply my ethics consistently to both myself and to others—thereby avoiding hypocrisy, which is integrity's opposite. If I think something is wrong for others to do, it's wrong for me to do, too.

What's awesome is that this doesn't just mean I'm more reliable and more honest with other people, it means I have to work on being more honest with myself. I struggle with depression and perfectionism, and they are inveterate liars. Perfectionism says that what's okay for others isn't okay for me, that what's admirable in others is the bare minimum for me. Depression says that there's no point trying to do better, because things will never improve, and anyway, everybody hates me forever and I'm going to die alone under a bridge. (Depression has some very over-the-top ideas.)

Integrity means that I hear those parts of myself and treat them the way I try to treat other people—with compassion, but without coddling. I say to them, "I hear you, and I understand why you feel that way, but that's not true." In some ways, this is a bazillion times harder than having integrity in my dealings with other people, but it's just as important. If I have integrity with others but not with myself, I don't really have integrity at all, now do I?

You may be saying to yourself, "Well, that's all very interesting, Ealasaid, but what does this have to do with Paganism?"

The tools I use to work on having more integrity are by and large Pagan ones. I sit in meditation, I pray to my Gods for guidance and assistance, and—most importantly—I regard integrity as something sacred. I believe we as humans are supposed to move toward integrity. It's part of our purpose.

Integrity isn't a duty laid on me by a vengeful God who has a lot of rules about how I have to act; it isn't a way for me to escape to a better plane of existence after I die. It's a goal for this lifetime.

Emphasis on "goal" there. Nobody has perfect integrity all the time. We all lose our tempers, fail to meet deadlines we said we would, flake out on friends, and so on. Nobody is perfect. Integrity doesn't demand that we be perfect, it demands that we keep trying.

O Sensei, the founder of Aikido, said: "My students think I don't lose my center. That is not so; I simply recognize it sooner, and get it back faster."

That's what I'm striving for: to see when I am sliding out of alignment and get back quickly, and to be compassionate toward my own imperfections as well as with those of others. That's integrity.

Fierce Compassion

"Fierce compassion" is a concept I think I first learned about from Thorn. The idea with fierce compassion is that you have compassion, but don't let it make you put up with things you shouldn't. As with a lot of things in my studies with Thorn, the trick is finding the middle ground—in this case, between idiot compassion on one hand (a.k.a. being a codependent doormat) and strictness or discipline without compassion on the other.

Compassion can mean seeing the weakness in others and empathizing with it, because I have weakness myself—and fierce compassion means not letting the weakness of others run roughshod over me. A related aphorism Thorn often quotes from Victor Anderson is, "Do not coddle weakness." She often adds, "Do not punish weakness."

The way I see it, fierce compassion comes from having compassion for others, but being fierce about my boundaries.

Boundaries are vital to mental, physical, and spiritual health. Boundaries are what let me make my own decisions rather than letting my parents, manager, friends, or partner choose for me. Boundaries are what help me say "No" to plans that would overextend me and damage my health. Boundaries are what help me spot hypocritical or otherwise unhealthy spiritual leaders and avoid them.

Fierce compassion helps me behind the wheel on my way to and from work every day—I have compassion for the other drivers on the road, which helps me not get really angry at them when they drive badly. I mean, I can remember lots of times I've been absent-minded or distracted (or pissed off!) behind the wheel. Fiercely defending my boundaries means that I expect other people to merge properly, that I take my turn when I have the right of way at a stop sign, that I call 911 when I see someone driving unsafely. It helps on a lot of fronts—my stress level is reduced, the stress level of my passengers is reduced, and hopefully the road is a little safer. Every time I let someone in ahead of me and they wave their thanks, I imagine that they'll be less likely to drive like a douchebag later.

Of course, as with integrity, I have to apply the same approach to myself as I do toward others. I have to have self-compassion as well as compassion for others. I can't be harder on myself than on other people. As a recovering perfectionist, this is really difficult. I know how to be cruel and nasty to myself, to punish myself—that's how I got fabulous grades for years and years. It's also how I wound up with fibromyalgia.[1]

I can't coddle myself, either. That's a good way for me to just stay in bed all day—which, appropriately, is just as bad for my fibro as trying to be perfect all the damn time. Again, it's the balance that makes for the best outcome. Compassion means not being nasty to myself, and fierceness means having enough discipline to do the things I need to get done.

It's a difficult balance to strike, between compassion and fierceness. Obviously, I don't get it right all day, every day. It's an ongoing process—and one to which I have to bring fierce compassion for myself. There's no sense beating myself up for failing to act with enough fierce compassion!

Love / Reverence for the Sacred

29. For I am divided for love's sake, for the chance of union.
30. This is the creation of the world, that the pain of division is as nothing, and the joy of dissolution all.

...

Love is the law, love under will.

— *Liber AL vel Legis, The Book of the Law*

I have a natural reverence for the sacred. There are certain sacred sites that automatically make me lower my voice a bit, make me reach mentally and energetically for something beyond myself. I feel that way both in enormous cathedrals and out in nature in general, especially in redwood groves (nature's cathedrals!). It's easy to feel reverent, to be filled with awe and love, in places that are obviously filled with divinity, places where lots of other people have spent time communing with deity.

That said, as a panentheistic pagan, I believe that the entire fabric of the universe is part of the divine—there is no thing which is not of God Herself. It's important to me to remember that everything is sacred. Every atom in existence is a part of God Herself. Every place is as sacred as a redwood grove, as a circle of standing stones, as a blessed spring. Every person is God Herself made manifest—even people I don't like.

It's amazing how much more clear right action becomes when I keep that in mind. How can I be horrible or hateful to someone if I remember that they are sacred? How can I support a company that treats its workers badly? Those workers are sacred. I wouldn't support a company that, say, damages churches, so how can I support one that damages its workers, who are no less holy?

I don't believe a person's actions are automatically sacred, just because I believe all people are sacred. When we become disconnected from each other, when we forget that love is the law, we do harm. It's important to me to prevent as much harm as I reasonably can—without doing more harm myself. That's why I study Aikido instead of one of the many other martial arts out there. Aikido is the Way of Harmony, the Way of Love. In Aikido we are taught that to harm our attacker is harming ourselves. Our goal is always to end conflict without harming anybody. If harm is necessary, we try to keep it to a minimum—no harm to ourselves and very specific harm to our attackers (if you examine most Aikido techniques, you will find that they tend to do irreversible damage to joints, thus disabling a person but not killing them. If an Aikidoka puts you down, you stay down, and likely won't be able to attack someone else in the future, either.).

This isn't easy, of course. Once we learn as infants that we are separate from the world around us, once we take that duality to heart, it's very, very difficult to get that nondualist worldview back. It's tempting to yell at other drivers, to gossip behind people's backs, to be cruel to others.

But we are all connected, and when I remember that connection, I remember love. I remember to love, to love everyone. (Sound familiar? A lot of major religions have commandments to love other people.) If I love everyone with the fierce compassion I was talking about before, that's really the only guide I need. Love is easily one of the simplest guidelines out there, and that's why it's one of my core values.

Love is the law, after all.

Of course, the other half of that is, "Love under will"…

Will / Self-Knowledge (a.k.a. Doing the Work)

Love is the law, love under will.
> — *Liber AL vel Legis, The Book of the Law*

Eight words the Wiccan Rede fulfill,
An it harm none do what ye will.
> — Doreen Valiente

The concept of "Will" (which I'm going to refer too with the capitalized "W" here, for clarity) is a big one in paganisms influenced by the fabulous Aleister Crowley, whose *Book of the Law* I've quoted above. See also the Wiccan Rede. Lots of people like to interpret Will as "whatever you want," but it's actually more specific.

The idea is that each person has a purpose, a reason for being here—their Will. It's what, once they know themselves thoroughly, they really want to do with their lives, what they feel drawn to. Figuring this out requires self-knowledge and contact with one's higher self / GodSoul / divine nature. The process of attaining contact with one's higher self, learning your Will, and accomplishing it is collectively referred to in many schools of thought as The Great Work—emphasis on the word "work." This is not a project for an armchair magician.

Doing the work is vital. You can't find your Will by reading about it; you have to actually keep up a daily practice, to sit your ass down and meditate even when you're tired or bored (or scared shitless. People seem to discount how terrifying to the ego sitting meditation can be.), to keep practicing ritual and magic until you know what you're doing, and so on.

This idea of constant self-improvement, of the need to find one's purpose, is at the heart of my ongoing work. It's what helps me to keep coming back to my daily practice, even after I've fallen out of the habit for a while. It's what helps me to keep working to be healthy enough to go to Aikido practice regularly.

Interwoven with the other values I've written about here, Will becomes the piece that ties them all together. The drive to find my Will is what keeps me seeking to have more integrity, to be fiercely compassionate, to be filled with love, and to filter all this through my pragmatic lens.

In Conclusion

These are my values, a summary of both how I see the world and how I try to operate in it. I certainly don't think they're the One True Way™ or a mandate for everyone to follow. But this is how the world looks from inside my head.

I'm glad the Pagan Values Blogging Month project exists, because I'm intrigued to read about how the world looks from inside other people's heads—and because the process of figuring out what, exactly, to write about was extremely illuminating. Regardless of whether you're pagan or not, dear reader, I hope you'll take some time to think about what your own values are. What does the world look like from inside *your* head?

---

[1] There's some evidence that extreme or continued trauma to the body (like a horrible car accident, a bad case of the flu, or constant adrenal depletion and chronic sleep deprivation) is correlated with developing fibromyalgia. I lived in a constant state of fight-or-flight maintained by too much caffeine and not enough sleep for years and years—and now I have fibro. It may not be accurate to say that I gave it to myself, but my symptoms sure get a hell of a lot worse if I slide back into those bad old habits!

Embodiment:
Ethics and Episteme

by Kevin Faulkner

The fundamental imperative of a Mystery School is to develop those within its doors upon every front. Every initiate brings some combination of powers and weaknesses, and all must be tried and improved, especially where the candidate lacks strength or practice. Some must master the lessons of silence, others of speech; some must gain strength, others suppleness; some must learn to be vulnerable, others fierce. Centering ourselves, we learn to tap the fundamental organs and cycles of generation behind creation, providing us the power and grace to find, test, and expand our growing edges within our bodies and our environments.

As the cycles of time endlessly turn, we invest ourselves more deeply into the dance of creation and destruction. We learn to better hear the tune, and we dance with more confidence and abandon. We trust our instincts, our learned skills, the rush of our passion, and our soft, absolute intuitive knowing. As the cycles turn, we also turn, revisiting our Selves, our Shadows, our sacred wounds, our growing edges. We revisit the skills and powers of life like water eddying into a rock, force and form reflecting one another more perfectly with every turning of the Wheel.

As an ecstatic, world-affirming tradition, we constantly remind ourselves to return to Earth. "This body, this Earth is my home" is first a mantra and later a holy exclamation of lived experience and embodied knowing. This is one of my greatest lessons within the container of Morningstar Mystery School. An academic and a nerd by temperament, and encouraged by my Mother in my natural intuition, I was reactionarily averse to most matters of the body. Hiding my own characteristics of gender and sexuality in the closet only reinforced this pattern.

"Ours is not a transcendental vision. Spirit is immanent. Embodied." Ours is a liberatory mystery, close kin to Reclaiming and Feri Witches. America's religious majority might ask "What book do you get your morals from?" Freeing ourselves from superstitious fear and slavery morality, we might begin to wonder, "What ARE the rules?" As thinking and feeling co-participants with the Great Mother, bound by no rede or book, we ask ourselves what makes right action. We bind ourselves to the pursuit of pursue positive virtues, which we envision, develop and embody through Pentacle and energetic work, introspection, and demon management.

As practitioners of magic, the stakes are raised. Oral histories abound of practitioners swept away by their "ego," in the pop-Buddhist sense, and living embarrassing lives until death-by-hubris. As our development progresses, we may find that the manifestation of thoughts becomes hazardously easy, and we are no longer responsible only to ourselves for controlling the currents of our minds. Hefting the tools honed in pursuit of our ecstatic Pagan theurgy, we delve bodily into the process and practice of ethics. Using our elemental/directional model as one of many useful ways to divide the experienced universe into interacting parts, patterns, and processes, we can attempt to think rigorously through the questions of ethics and develop some frameworks for understanding.

We begin in the North, for the measure of all magic is matter. Spiritual vision that cannot translate into better living is a liability, as running a stronger current than they are equipped to handle will fail. If one holds that magic can impact the material sphere, one should be able to provide results. If one believes magic is all "in the head," then it is merely so much idle delusion and fantasy if the head and life of the practitioner are not clearly benefited by the practice. Functionality is the great conundrum of magic, that we who practice so "superstitious" an art may reject that which does not work as "superstition" and accept that which does work as the occult action of natural law, also known as "magic." Why would these strange and mysterious practices continue across cultures and millennia if they were so much self-delusion and trickery?

The realm of Earth is where we consider the origin and end of ethics: Results. Impacts. Outcomes. This is not to begin with that the ends justify the means, but rather that "The means create the ends." Consideration of our impacts, intentional and unintentional, must guide our ethical decisions.

"But what of our intentions?!" People love "good intentions," because everyone believes they have them. The parent throwing a queer child onto the street might be showing "tough love" in the face of what they've been taught to imagine is tremendous sin and peril. But intentions can derail in practice. I can want to help you take care of yourself and infantilize you until you no longer remember how to live your own life. You can intend to offer comfort but deepen my panic and anxiety. Causing pain with good intentions is perhaps more forgivable than doing so with obnoxiousness as your goal, but only if you then choose to learn behavior that is better suited to reach the end in heart.

The willingness to listen, learn, and change is at the core of adaptability. A healthy sense of Pride means understanding both our largeness and our smallness; our skills and powers as well as our deficits and struggles. Healthy Pride is healthy Humility; accepting the truth of others' differences and allowing others to speak, think, and choose for themselves. Astrology has helped me in this regard. By naming differences, I can better comprehend them, instead of assuming that others are making different decisions due to some form of ineptitude.

When we attend to the world and listen ever more deeply, we begin to form and refine mental models of how the universe works. Traditional magical and cosmological paradigms are such models, as are empirical science and political ideologies such as dialectical materialism. Different models have different strengths. Empirical science is structurally useful for determining the general principles of controllable, repeatable systems. Dialectical materialism has more power as a political narrative than as an iron-clad framework for understanding historical forces. Metaphysical models help us to think about and imagine the world in manageable chunks and graspable patterns (as in this essay), and in doing so provide a sort of psychic image-map or talking-board that enables communication between realms or planes in which consciousness operates and "speaks" very differently.

These are the Eastern, Air powers: the breath of life, observation, communication, rational discourse, discrimination, exploration, and paradigm-building. Living our lives, we can observe how how our behavior impacts ourselves and one another. This is the beginning of the formation of an ethics. This dovetails with our epistemological approach, which can be summarized by the wise words of Victor Anderson to "experience first and believe later." This is quite distinct from the religious imperative shared by so many of the "peoples of the book" who often insist upon right belief and orthodox profession of faith as central to religion and morality. This distinction is relevant because moral and, by extension, ethical systems in Western culture are largely derived from the logic of the major mono-religions. Many raised in such faith traditions may habitually ask first what we ought to believe, or expect a divine authority to dictate clear laws on moral, ethical, and metaphysical matters. Responsibility to internalize our own locus of authority can at first be terrifying. But if we learn to listen, we may allow our Shaping to serve the greater vision and tapestry of Life, and we recognize that responsibility as the beautiful and sacred trust it truly is.

As understanding grows from observation of our embodied selves, we begin to see the cycles and movements of energies throughout the world and yearn to merge our creative spark with them. Dedicated to the complete unfolding of our highest human potential, we may come to know that a reflection of the heart of God Herself is the substance of every human Spirit, seeking to create and be known, and add beauty to the world, even as at the primal moment She shattered "for love's sake, for the hope of union."

We hold our desire, our sexual-sensual nature, our creative spark as a guide and sacred trust. From these, we see how we may reach out our hands and bring forth such flowers in our Mother's Endless Garden as will enhance beauty and life, offering new smells of love, intoxication, and enchantment for all the other children, alive and yet to come, in this wild and yet all-too-weary world. This spell beautifies us, too, and we do not allow vanity and false pride to stop it, for "In adorning itself, the rose adorns the garden." As Priests or Priestesses cultivating health in our relationships with our bodies, environments, and resources, this beauty manifests in the Earth realm around us. We start not with questions of limitation and negation, but ask: How may we be of service to the Most Beautiful Vision?

This is the power of intention, of will, and of desire, mediated through the Southern Fire. This is the place of that holy intention, where desire transforms the simple contact of hands into holy healing. Desires for love and healing are holy and wholesome, but our intentions can be expressed in toxic and counterproductive ways if we fail to heed new information from the east and operate from calcified belief systems, constantly assuring ourselves "I know best." Overly exuberant sexuality, naïve to the power of sex, can result in awkward or traumatic experiences; well-intended and enthusiastic advice can feel violent or dismissive to someone desperate to feel *heard*.

Our intention, informed by the eastern powers, finds its quenching and containment in the Western Waters. The Air capacity of communication is echoed here in the West's receptive capacity of deep listening. More deeply attuned to the words (Air) and spirit (Fire) of our interactions with other beings, we swim more fully and more mindfully in the waters of relationship. Here, in the wet realms preceding those of Earth, we approach again the physical but linger first in the flowing tides of emotion and the moon-pulled oceans. Knowledge of Eastern and Southern powers informs our awareness of the unique ways these flowing souls move in and about every human's mind, body, and emotions.

Recognizing every creature as a unique combination of forces flowing in its own pattern, we increasingly come to know things wordlessly, directly, intuitively. We enter relationship, swimming together in the shifting tides of light flowing forth in kaleidoscopic prisms from the deep primordial word. Our ethics, manners, and aesthetics become more intertwined as we come to see beauty in harmony and active balance, and seek the most elegant ways to dance with even the most potent, chaotic energies with which the universe may present us.

These urgings and promptings and inner knowings become obvious to us because of our practice of embodiment. The power of Earth not only anchors our ethical considerations into real-world patterns and impacts but also reminds us that our body is a powerful ethical tool. Yes, it can become excited or enraged and difficult to control; we are an animal, after all. But that is the point: Do not our hearts burn and our stomachs churn when we witness injustice? Don't our hands long to offer aid when we see others in labor?

During my years in the closet, I either misdirected or actively lied to maintain my "secret." My body helped force out the truth; not because my flounce emerged, but because my body dislikes to lie. When I lie, my whole organism responds as though something icky just happened. Communication within the Self opens tremendously when we train our intellectual, Talking Soul to listen to our physical body and emotional, Animal Soul. With increased communication, we are more able to harmonize internally and externally. The emotional and intuitive processes of the West connect with the physical and survival processes of the North. The body responds positively to truth, and sickens from a lie. (One more example being the "toxic mimics" produced by our industrialized food system.)

As experience, consideration, digestion, relationship, and inspiration turn within our souls, we develop the pearl of true wisdom: the capacity for right action in untried circumstances. In our earliest days we must begin to learn ethics by trial and error, sculpted by the considerations and teachings of our elders, but with time we discover how the uniqueness of every moment is a reflection of fundamental universal patterns. As our emotional and intellectual bodies become still, these organs of vibration and communication learn also to receive information. We begin to find ourselves openly, spontaneously choosing right action. We walk with mindless luck through a minefield, speaking and moving from a deeper wisdom than one to which we can lay claim.

With that, we return to the Earth in North, the realm of action, digestion, silence. We learn and we act. The cycle cannot be divorced from itself; no one phase is in isolation. Listening to our own hearts and guts, deeply rooted in compassion, we learn to trust ourselves and our judgments without laws clearly prescribed by an ancient or modern lawgiver. We see when our intentions are good, and we strive for honesty when we are tempted by self-service or superficial convenience, for we esteem too highly our integrity and self-possession to compromise it by the willful entertainment of un-truth.

Claiming our locus of authority and embracing the powers of the directions requires us to take responsibility. We must take the lead in setting the boundaries necessary to contain and facilitate our creative, transformative power. We must remain rooted in Earth in our exchanges with our Gods, for—as Thorn reminds us often—they rarely understand the details of physicality. Many atrocities have been committed because someone's crazed imagination or a passing astral nasty has posed as a sufficiently convincing message from God. Some believe that Jehovah's test of Abraham in the matter of his son was a failed test, for the sacrifice was interrupted: "I desire mercy, not sacrifice!!"

Our Pagan epistemology and our Pagan ethics must come together to the table. Many of us relish our capacity for direct relationship with our Powers: the Gods, Ancestors, Land Spirits and many others. The active, living participation with the co-creative web of life is the beating heart of appeal, healing, and power in our traditions. But this vast and unorthodox source of knowledge is not without drawbacks, and human error can prove egregious. Many in our society believe that humans need an external moral force to guide their actions, but many of history's darkest moments happened in subservience to exactly such an idea. People displace their loyalty onto a crown, a company, or a book, and they may believe those who have not are not truly human. They mistake the abstractions of the mind, Air, for the non-negotiable reality of Earth.

As Pagans, we encourage one another to treat information received by mystical means as we would that given by a lover, acquaintance, or confidante, and to develop trust with any source of information in just the same way. In ethical matters, we must be the final arbiter, for what is at stake are our souls, pride, and honor. As with all other matters, the realm of Earth provides the final test and proof. We are not here to serve the Gods; we are here to give thanks and honor to those who make our lives possible by using wisdom, compassion, and our sacred creative-sexual power to create a more beautiful world for those who shall inherit it from us.

Returning to our context, to our center, to our web of relationships, the power of Earth, presence, and embodiment reminds us that our behavior does not impact us alone. The grain, fowl, and plant roots that die for our dinner are as invested in our decisions as our ancestors. The center is not only one point, but three, a whirling axis upon which the entire mill of magic turns. From the Center, we see both Above and Below: the cosmic symmetry of electron clouds and superclusters as well as the

EMBODIMENT

broadening and deepening impulses that complete our array of possibility.

From the Center, we see in Earth the reality, the constraints and possibility, of all the life around us. We recognize our duties to the human web as well as the plants and animals that give us sustenance, the wind that fills our lungs, the trees who breathe with us in the sexual dance of respiration between the red-blooded and the green. Rocks, clouds, and every expression of movement upon this planet interrelate. Acknowledging our smallness and impotence in the face of cosmic vastness, we must also acknowledge our power to destroy. Our responsibility may be greatest for what is nearest, but there is no horizon line we may draw to say, "Here my responsibility ends." All That Is depends upon All That Is. When we critique the cosmic vision-in-action, what we are most likely to demonstrate is only our own arrogance. Returning again and again to center and invoking the higher perspective and wisdom of our Divine Souls, which is God Herself incarnate through Us, we see beyond our immediate interests and perspectives to a more beautiful and noble path. This path is determined by our unique skills, passions, values and placement within the limitless tapestry which is She. We learn to get out of our own way. We cease to resist and cling when our intentions are imperfectly manifested, but own up to our choices and mistakes and learn what we did that caused us to "miss the mark." We forgive ourselves and try again, resolved to do better.

Because, again, isn't that the test of matter? For us as magicians to come to know our lives as one magical act and to perfect our art of causing change in accordance with will? To beautify the worlds through the Philosopher's Stone of our lives? In such a lofty and potent art, we can afford no room for clinging to error, but must love and pursue truth, which is that web of reality knitting this Cosmos together.

Fiat Lux! (Erat Nox.)

The Stillness About Which the World Spins

by Anthony Rella

Human consciousness exists in the encounter between the inner and outer worlds. Discord and confusion arises when I mistake one world for the other. When the boundaries between the two are too loose, I struggle to function. When the boundaries are too rigid, life feels empty and void of purpose. When I cannot distinguish between the two, I feel anxiety and waste energy trying to control what is not within our sphere of power. To avoid the uncertainties of the outer world, I might retreat to the comforting mystery of the inner world. I might avoid feeling the fear within by commanding those around me to behave in a way that helps me to be at ease.

Cultural idioms convey an underlying push for endless, unsustainable effort to contain the underlying anxieties of living. We talk about trying to "juggle" the demands of life, "put out fires," "keep it together," or "stay on the ball." To feel that I am "on the ball" or that I've "got it together" has its pleasure: a sense of control over chaos. When life feels particularly good and successful, I feel a smug sense of superiority that worsens the sting when change reminds me that I can be as messy and un-together as I perceived others to be.

Within Tartarus, torturous realms are replete with images of fixed, repetitive, endless and unsatisfying labor. Sisyphus struggles to mount the boulder upon the rounded peak, praying that this time it will rest so finally he can relax, only to discover once again that it simply rolls back to the beginning. The Danaides attempt to fill a bath with jars who work against their purpose, emptying out before reaching their aim. Tantalus stretches for what will slake his craving, always beyond his reach. Such endless labor is addictive, and addiction is such endless effort. Constant stress and anxiety feed my ego's attachment to feeling needed, special, and important. Those who loudly claim they "don't want any drama" seem to be the ones who surround themselves with the most. Struggling to "keep it together," I rarely find a time in which "it" is not threatening to come apart. Times of relative peace are vaguely unsettling, as I become still enough to sense the hollowness beneath my daily action. My tendency is to avoid this discomfort and find a new distraction, but this tendency keeps me from truth seeking recognition.

I walk my dog and notice her fascinated sniffing. She urinates deliberately on this patch of grass and not this rock. She defecates and eats things off the ground, growls at other dogs and blissfully greets total strangers. Wholly engrossed in perception, she does her work in the outer world. My mind becomes adrift with recollections of last night's television show, tomorrow's needs, this morning's perceived insult, a fantasy of a time that will never occur, and this afternoon's desired outcome. Thoughts and feelings arise with a sense of urgency. Insisting upon attention, thoughts circulate and fail to change or resolve. The sudden snap and pull of my dog as she growls at another breaks the internal cycle. I do not thank her for bringing me to presence. I notice feelings of irritation, as though those thoughts and feelings, unlike the thousands of others before, could have been the ones to bring me to a critical insight that I had lacked before. Thinking about the life I am not living feels more important than the life before me in the moment. When will I have thought enough that I can finally let that boulder rest and enjoy the life that is here?

In *Jung and Tarot*, Sallie Nichols evokes this cycling through the Tarot symbol of the Wheel of Fortune. My inner world is a Wheel of spinning thoughts and feelings. Strapped to the edge of my personal Wheel, I might feel rolled flat one moment and exalted the next, lifted high into the air without a chance to breathe before being slammed again to earth. Without the steadying influence of discipline and a coherent sense of self, my life looks like a series of missed opportunities, failures, surprise fortunes, and causes for habituated feelings—not the ones I desire, but the ones I feel fated to have. Along the path I see the angel, the lion, the bull, the eagle as the issues I can never fully resolve; the ridiculing guardians of my torment. This hell is life spent on the edge of the personal Wheel. The hollowness I sense beneath the constant flow is the still, empty center of the Wheel. Spiritual work cultivates our inner movement toward that center. After so much drama, returning to stillness and empty space can feel like a welcome respite. Practice will strengthen that hub and give greater integrity to the Wheel.

When I was younger, I was so exhausted by endless pontificating and anxious ruminations that I wished to take a vacation from myself. Drugs scared me, so I gravitated toward meditation to stop the noise. I thought of mastery as the ability to regulate the self from an external position, able to the steer the wayward heart with detachment. I imagined fantastic powers of mind that could supersede the limitations of the body. I was identified with a limited part of myself, the intellect, and perceived the body as hostile terrain populated by alien forces, the emotions. The intellect protected its reign by violent exclusion and oppression of these threatening parts of self, unable to see that such tyranny was enslavement.

Now I consider surrender a path to mastery of the self. If I am unwilling to attend to the vicissitudes of my inner Wheel, then I deprive myself of the opportunity for knowledge. If I do not know the self, I cannot achieve mastery. Knowing the self means more than pointing to the identities we claim, our relationships, our thoughts and feelings, our personality tendencies, or our families. Recognizing the patterns of life is a step that can lead us toward seeing the underlying patterns of the patterns. I might say, "I always fall in love with someone who doesn't love me." That is a superficial story about the self. Is it really true? Why does it feel true? When does it feel true? When does it feel untrue?

Finding stillness does not require the abandonment of life, but rather a movement toward experience. I cultivate consciousness by observing how my inner Wheel spins in counterpoint to the outer Wheel. Suddenly I can notice how an ongoing conflict with a coworker resembles every other conflict I've had with this person. I have played this part many times: the wounded invisible victim who suffers in silent resentment, believing myself to be superior.

Other times I switch roles and play the villain. I try to get the lines just right and rehearse in my mind, but the play turns out the same every time. When I can see this compulsion to repetition for what it is, I can experiment with a new choice. If I no longer play my assigned role, then those around me cannot play theirs. Discomfort arises. I might feel pressured back into my old role through anger, sadness, manipulation, flattery, and temptation. My inner resolve might be tested by weariness or anxiety about the unpredictable future. Changes might also be met with encouragement, relief, and gratitude. These small changes to my inner being often seem to ripple out to inspire my peers and loved ones.

Those of us who have ever failed to change a habit, break an addiction, or leave a relationship might see that even relapse feels like a piece of the cycle. Truly seeing one's self can make us feel vulnerable to self-criticism and despair. Here spiritual practice can have its greatest benefits. I work to cultivate connection with my God Soul, the divine part of self that can witness and hold my entire being with love, compassion, and understanding. I succeed and God Soul holds me with love. I fail and God Soul holds me with love.

Daily practice provides the support I need to cultivate the center through which God Soul can enter awareness. The meditative act of sitting and bringing presence to breath is a foundational act of my practice. Doing so helps me to step away from the edge of the Wheel of endless reactivity. I make a deliberate effort to stop running and watch. When I sit physically still, I cannot evade the sensations of the body and activity of the heart and mind. Thoughts and feelings proliferate and pull me away from the task. I must choose to return attention to breath, sound, or sensation as meditative focus. This is the practice that leads us to silence. Many new students of meditation feel they are not doing meditation well if they cannot quiet their minds. Often students will give up or decide meditation does not work for them, dissatisfied with the lack of obvious results. I argue that perceiving that inner busyness and restlessness is the sign that meditation is working. I judge the quality of my practice by looking at the rest of my life. Do I feel more at ease? Do I find it easier to return to my center when problems arise? Do I feel more spaciousness in my life? Do I notice a difference between my experience before sitting and my experience after?

Beginning to recognize the inner Wheel, I can attend more clearly to my interactions within larger Wheels of economic boom and bust, cultural vacillation, cycles of history, the Wheel of the Year, and the movement of our planet around the sun. Cycles of days, months, and years bring us around to circumstances we might love or loathe. For me, the sun's entrance into Libra often brings forth a sense of futility and self-reproach. A voice insists I have been wasting my life and enviously looks to others' successes. Perhaps it is the harvest time that causes me to review what I am gathering into my life. Perhaps it is the sun's illumination of my natal Saturn, that old task-master.

Octavia Butler wrote, "God is change." Change is the action of Spirit, evoked by the the Wheel of Fortune as constant motion, constant change, but always cycling past recurrent themes. The eagle, angel, bull, and lion herald the change of seasons, the fixed elements that give structure to our experience, and the themes of history. When I first read Dostoevsky and Chekhov, I was amazed by how these 19th-century Russian writers seemed to be writing about themes and concerns that were relevant to my (at the time) 20th-century experience. The fashion of one decade is reviled in the following decade and revived in the next. History suggests ongoing movements between economic boom and bust, shifts between liberal expansion and conservative contraction. Even from this vantage of viewing history and human existence as a series of ongoing cycles, my mortal view is so limited that I cannot anticipate exactly what comes next. We can look to astrology to read the cosmic "clock" of celestial bodies, yet the sun in Libra of this year is unlike the sun in Libra of last, due to the shifting of so many other bodies. I cannot see whether the action I take today will result in success or failure, or failure today that tomorrow will be considered success.

As a Millennial child, much of my youth was spent in a time of relative affluence. I and my peers were often told how special we were and how we had the promise of achieving material success while following the truth of our hearts. Adulthood has confronted us with a constricted job market and reduced economic opportunities. I could not find work in my career and thought the failure was a reflection on myself, my inability to rise to the promise of my generation. Such thoughts paralyzed me from attempting to do anything else with my life. So I returned again to presence and the stillness at my center. Sitting with myself helped me to recognize that I can only act in integrity, shift my relationship to the worlds, and find my place within the patterns of the larger Wheel. Today I feel love, I believe myself to be successful, I am praised by my boss, and I return to my still center. Today I feel miserable, I believe everything I touch turns to shit, and I get yelled at by my boss and my lover, and I return to my still center.

I have shifted through cycles of feeling rejected, despising others, despising myself, feeling some accomplishment and wanting to believe life would be better forever, feeling disappointed when some misstep brought me back into defeat. Some days I have felt that the best I can manage is simply to survive the moment and hope something changes. We can do better than merely survive. Transformation is possible. The practice of witchcraft brings me out of my spinning thoughts and into relationship with the movement of nature and the cosmos. When I work with the rotations of the moon, I begin to feel orb's ebb and pull on the tides within, and notice how others around me seem to be working through similar problems. Now I feel connected to the tides of the ocean and the struggles of those around me. Now I no longer feel alone with my private suffering, or my longing for freedom.

Taking time each day to sit in stillness, I open and bless the space that is the center of my inner self. Once so painful, I find that emptiness to be the hollow of a singing bowl. The motion of drama, boredom, pleasure, and pain need no longer be a source of distress but rather the catalyzing mallet that circumambulates the sacred center. Consciously experiencing the spinning within and without, my self emanates a soothing tone, a note that offers peace.

~ Gnosis ~

Dragon

by Sean McMahon

Presence

by Elfin

Circling in a globe of stars,
Rocked gently in the cradle of heaven.
There is no time but now,
No place but the All,
No self, only presence.

The kiss, the touch, the entering;
Resistance and surrender.
A portal opened, love entering,
A soul opens, bounds dissolving,
Swept into Presence.

God Hirself,
The curved mirror, the black bowl,
The Is and I Am;
The first love, reflected eternally
Reverberating.

Circling in the echoes of love,
Cradled in the endless song.
God Is, We Are, I Am,
Each reflecting the other,
Gifts poured from heaven's bowl.

Dark Heart

by Elfin

The heart
is a rough black stone.
A bit of star-stuff,
sooty and smoky,
scorched and burn't on its long fall to earth.
Which speaks,
in accusations:

> "You'll never be pretty enough"
> "You shouldn't have done that"
> "You're too quick to anger, too quick to fear"
> "Now look what you've done!"

The heart
beats within our lover.
Hear it:

"What a beautiful person"
"I love what my lover does"
"How graceful!"
"I adore you"

The heart
beats within you
Feel it:
beating
Pulsing with life
beating
Growing quicker
beating
at your lover's touch
beating
Pumping
beating
the waters of life
beating
in each of us

Some of the dust
falls away.

The heart
Knows.

Breathe deeply,
Feel your body:

Gravity's pull
Slow breaths
Energy all about
The world felt (but unseen)

The heart
holds a bright fire.
Close your sight-eyes
And feel with your heart.
Your lover's heart:
beating
The beauty inside
pulsing
Feeding every cell
feeding
Spreading warmth

glowing

The heart
can see.

Make love, sing, and see:
yourself
reflected in your lover's caress
yourself
as the beloved sees you
yourself

in a mirror that sees no falsehood
yourself
in a way that brings no blame
yourself
as the Goddess sees you.
The heart
Can heal.

The rough-hewn heart cracks
Pieces break, slough, and tumble
Away.

The heart
Awakens.

Hold yourself,
make love,
And look in the mirror:
yourself
Beautiful
yourself
As the Goddess made you
yourself
A piece of star-stuff
yourself
fallen to earth
yourself
and brought to light.

Dark Heart

The heart is a sparkling stone
Of polished black obsidian.

The Star Goddess saw herself
In the infinite curved black mirror of space
and fell in love
And created Miria, all of us, from that perfection
and fell in love
And from their union came the Blue God, playful
and fell in love
And from their union came the Green God, creative
and fell in love
And from their union came the Red God, passionate hunter
and fell in love
And they danced together
and fell in love
Until the whole of creation fell back into the star goddess again
and fell, in love.
Her heart, perfect, shining, black, infinite
Forged in love.
Her heart,
Is also yours.
Which fell (to earth)
In love.

Death, Remembrance, and Love

by Rynn Fox

My grandmother is dying.

I have this memory. I am four. I am singing "Skidamarink." Perhaps you know the song. Its lyrics are simple:

Skidamarink a-dink, a-dink,
Skidamarink a-doo,
I love you.
I love you in the morning,
And in the afternoon;
I love you in the evening,
And underneath the moon.
Oh, skidamarink a-dink, a-dink,
Skidamarink a-doo,
I love you.

She is beaming with pride and recording me on a cassette tape as I sit on the kitchen counter. I feel a swelling of pride. She hugs me. I hug her, gripping her tightly; my arms still chubby with baby fat. My head pressed to her breastbone.

If I had listened hard enough, I would have heard her heartbeat.

I've been watching people die since I was four. I've buried 22 people. Some were classmates, others teachers, but most have been family. Not extended family, but close family. It's shaped my practice as a witch, my relationship with my spirits, and my family.

My grandmother knows I'm a witch, a devil worshiper. I don't mind her categorization. The Gods of one religion are often the demons of another. It also hasn't lessened her love of me in any way. She doesn't consciously know that I work with the dead, or the living about to left behind. But she seems to understand this unconsciously.

"Erin Morgan…"

"Yes, Grandma."

"I need you to help me organize my jewelry for you girls after I die."

"Are you sure you don't want to have us all over and make us mud wrestle for them? It'd be funny. You'd laugh."

She ignores my comment and gingerly pulls out her jewelry box, necklaces and earrings coiled haphazardly within. I pull out a clip-on earring and notice her inhale sharply. I look up and consider her face. It's pinched with the realization that the things you hold precious maybe junk to someone else.

"You girls have pierced ears. I guess you won't want that."

With my free hand I pull up my shirt and tuck it under my bra while my other hand opens and closes the earring clasp on the base of my bra. I shimmy for her.

"I can use this, Grandma. See?" I keep shimmying. "It'll be fantastic for belly dancing."

She gives me a wry smile. We both know what I'm trying to do. Can't outrun death. Can't avoid it. But we can laugh at it. Nothing to do but laugh until we cry and cry until we laugh again.

"I have something for you."

I watch her shuffle to one of her drawers and I follow her. She pulls out a cherry-red box and opens it.

"These are opals from Australia. They're yours. I haven't worn them since your grandfather passed. You can get them remounted if you don't like how I had them done."

"They're beautiful."

"Good. They're yours now."

There are many things left unsaid between us. Understandings that I think we need to come to before she passes. But this is her death. It's her process, not mine. She is living in the process of dying. My place is to help her. I'm struggling to help her where she'll let me. I'm also trying as much as I can to remember.

Because what is remembered, lives.

My grandfather is standing next to my sister. Their necks are craned with hands shielding eyes from the blistering desert sun. My grandmother exits the RV and walks to my grandfather and sister. She follows their eye-line to me. I am ten and am halfway up a 150-foot sandstone cliff trying to get my sister's kite where it's wedged into the rock face. The rock, being sandstone, crumbles in my hands with too much pressure. Same with my precarious footholds. I can see her in my peripheral vision. Barely.

There are hushed expletives in her feathery voice. She asks my grandfather what the hell…and is cut off as my grandfather explains the situation. I can hear the fear spiked with anger in her voice. She questions my grandfather's sanity and abandons her argument with him. Her voice rings out, echoing through Red Rock Canyon. I am now five feet from the kite. "Erin Morgan! Get down here NOW!"

"I can't!" I shout over my shoulder. "I'm almost to the kite!" I reach the kite. It's only then I remember I don't know how to go down. I look at my family over my shoulder. My grandfather's and sister's faces are unreadable. But not my grandmother's. Her face is lined with worry and fear.

Even now I can hear her silent prayer: "Please God, don't let her fall; please God, don't let her fall."

I didn't fall.

What is remembered, lives.

It's a simple enough phrase, yet for me, it contains rich concepts that we only mine in the face of the enigma of Death. Even then the path to understanding was only opened when I chose to open the door and walk the path the words laid before me. Contained within those words are a type of grace, a spell, a binding, a life, a death, a reconnection, an undertaking, a renewal, an awareness. It's this last word, awareness, that contains the spark of possibility in the face of Death. When I opened to it fully, this awareness was voluminous and multifaceted.

Death, like life, is a process. A series of moments, memories, and events; some planned, others unplanned, all are weathered. It's through remembering that my beloved dead live again within me. It's through the act of remembering that I bring the lessons of the past with me. It's how I make sense of the senseless by reframing old memories with new eyes and understandings. But I had to do it with intention. Remembering in this way has helped me see my ancestors as the flawed humans they are and hold them with compassion. This in turn has helped me increase the compassion I hold for myself. And the love. It's in doing this work that I've realized that when I heal myself, somehow the dead are also healed. Maybe it's because when the cycle of unintentional and intentional wounds that are passed from generation to generation is stopped, they can let go of their guilt and forgive themselves. Maybe it's because love can move back in time to heal a broken heart. If you have had the magical experience that says all space and time is here and now, then this is certainly possible. Maybe it's because all the ballads are true: that love is the only thing that survives.

"Your parents never told me that." My grandmother's face is contorted with worry, concern, and pain. "Why didn't they tell me?"

I had just told her of a harrowing experience that left its indelible mark on me. She'd wanted to know why I acted a certain way. So I told her.

"What could you have done, Grandma?"

"I could have loved you more."

"Oh, Grandma, you love me enough already."

And I want to hold on to her love. It's flawed and it's human, but it'll be the only thing I'll have left when she

Death, Remembrance, and Love

passes. Because her love, and her flaws and grace, are a part of the fabric of me. Because I need that love to carry me through life and eventually my own death. I want to pass on that love, too. I want that love to be remembered, to leave its indelible imprint on me and my descendants. Maybe it's the only way we achieve true immortality.

Because what is remembered, lives.

The Hinges

by Litha

The Great Wheel: Seasons

Dark December mornings sleep
In August's bliss
The golden light, the welcoming air
Enfold the place at Winter's heart
Awaiting
Awakening

Each season calls the others,
Whispering
Of beauty and desire.

Samhain: Roses in the Kitchen

Last night Freddie brought flowers. Roses, six.
A different color, each.

I put them in a glass vase upon the kitchen table
And Michael lit candles. And David came downstairs
With photos to share

In the candlelight, the roses glowed with borrowed light
Then Selchie arrived with Doug and a bottle of wine
I got out glasses. We opened and poured

And, in the early evening of a rainy fall night,
I looked at the roses and thought,
This must be it
—the meaning of life.

Yule: Snow Ponies

The snow ponies are flying today
Snowflakes fat as my nose plaster my eyes shut with
    cold kisses
The Snow Queen is laughing in the winter wind
The hearthfire lit at home

Fearless, I walk through the blizzard
Listening for the bells of her magnificent sleigh
Somewhere, the Great Bear rests in an icy cave
Amid all her shining stars
I have no doubts

This, all of it
The snow, the cold, the ice, the fire, the shining stars
Her wild unbroken laughter
The bells, the ponies, the Mysteries, Her hand on my
    back

My warm home

Candlemas: The Snake

I had almost forgotten the python
I once held her in my arms,
Her smooth skin, how gently she moved
Her careful weight against my breasts
Her keeper said,
You are warm
And, also
She loves us

Today it was the river
I wanted to hold her in my arms
Her depth, the breadth of her
The shock of her cold water
On my heart

To bend my ear close
To her water,
To hear her icy murmurs
And to whisper back
Of love

Eostar: For Rilke

The wind curves an arm round my sheltering home
Hurls howling lashings of rain, great splatters from
    out of
an opening fist
Lightning cracks down

Rain drops whisper at windows, long soft slidings
Gathered on glass, descending to ground

Forgive all   forget nothing

Descend, back bent toward the grey spent sky
Collect all that is sweetest, like bees

As in springtime, making all seem like new
How snowdrops spring forth

Like rain, run down, soak in and spread
Sustenance, succour, the sprouting of seeds

Or last night the moon's glance
Lighting my way to benediction, release

My cat returns home, comes in from the rain
Fur damp from the storm, whiskers jeweled with dew,
    leaving behind
Early morning offering
Bloodied and headless, a mouse dead on the porch

Red cardinal carols one liquid note
Singing to this, most blessed of days,

Know grace   grasp ecstacy
Spring's lullaby to winter is eleison to all the stars

Beltane: The Faery Queen's Earth Song

I dwell with the Faery Queen these days
Each morning she awakens me, her singing
Calls me back to Earth

Forever changed

Enchanted, I see
One shimmering raindrop nested
In sudden bloom of pink and blue forget me not

Arrested. The lilac
Halts me with fragrance, offers
Her delicious embrace and

Time stands still. Almost I forget to enter
My own backdoor

Bird sounds in morning

Down the lane, the ancient elm mutters softly
I hear him as if there were
No other sound

My skin warm to my own touch
Softly fleshed, my older body is
Looser, stiffer, than was once   I am still

Human

In the park across the street, some children play
Mothers watch, babies are comforted, young lovers
    hold hands

It is a warm afternoons of spring's return
My heart is filled with grief and love

Resilient, this world carries on. Each morning I follow
The Faery Queen's song, her luring me back
To Earth

Litha: Great Bear

we headed out in the boat in the night
across the dark water, between the shoals,
under sky that was nothing but stars, almost.
And I saw meteors showering down above us and
northern lights on the horizon beside us,
in colors and everywhere, stars stars stars.

Melanie saw nothing but the water in front of us, terrified
we would hit a shoal in the dark, though
she knows those waters intimately, has been going there all of her life and,
despite her fears, remembered everything
perfectly, picking out each rock and buoy and place marker with her flashlight,
all along the way, with impeccable accuracy.
The next morning, a bear swam by across the channel in front of the cottage, accompanied by a loon

Each thing is contained within its opposite.
No wonder I am confused

Mother of Wisdom, the breath and the flame, let your light move through me. May I see clearly.

Mother of Compassion, the chalice and star, let your love move through me. Let my heart be open.

Mother of Spirit, the cauldron of souls, come into my centre. Let your will be mine.

Lammas: Golden Apples

The dog likes to walk in the village
Sniffing for yesterday's child-dropped ice cream
And the sentinel signs
On posts and plants and walls
Of other early day dogs

But I want to turn,
Crossing the bridge, walking past the old factory
Through these woods
To the steep rock-walled path
And down to the river where I throw myself in,
Naked and singing
To the aromatic green of the cedar-lined banks
And the brown pull of cool water
Across my sorrowing body
And the dog, knee-deep, watching
In the unencumbered morning solitude
Of this graceful place

Today, it is summer
Too cold, almost, to swim
But I do
Suddenly, along the path of my shivering return
The way is strewn with apples
Tumbling, small and golden at my feet

The air filled with sweet fragrance
In all the times I have come here
I never saw until now
The ancient generous tree
At the top of the path.

Mabon: For Bonnie

Among angels, I am the fallen one.

Fallen to earth.

Am I a fool for remembering
Once, these wings could fly?

Demons, Dreams, and Visions: Connecting Morningstar and Shamanic Work

by Annette Rath-Beckmann

Dreams

In my personal work towards self-possession there is a close connection between themes from our Morningstar homework agenda and important dreams and visions that show up simultaneously. I have noticed several examples of this kind of interaction. In June 2012, Thorn asked my cohort, "How are you doing with your demon work?" This question took me by surprise, and I wondered "Why demon work?" Were there any demons who impeded my work towards self-possession and integration? I had not thought of demons for some time and did not know how to approach this piece of homework.

I remembered a strong dream that occurred at the time of May 2012's New Moon, during which I had an encounter with one of my (external) personal demons: my father, who died 15 years ago. In this dream, I had thrown him out of a family home by yelling at him and telling him to get out of my life for good. He left the house but turned around and said, "I'll be back." In my dream and waking life, I knew that yelling and cursing were no adequate means to heal a relationship, but speaking my mind aloud without restriction had felt good.

During the afternoon of the day of my dream, I used the New Moon energy to separate from my father by means of a shamanic journey.

For this journey, I went to my special place for soul retrieval directly underneath the summit of a very high mountain. It was a dark night without moonlight but with many stars twinkling in the sky. The mountain summit was partly hidden by foggy clouds. My father and I were sitting opposite to each other in the two halves of an "eight" that was built by blue fire. In my half of the "eight," my animals of power were supporting me; the big black spider that is part of my shamanic power was above me. We started rattling, and suddenly there was my old cat Socke, who had died in April 2012. Socke separated the two halves with his paw. Immediately, in his half of the "eight," my father vanished into the universe.

The scene changed, and I was in the home of my great-aunt on my mother's side, together with my great-grandmother, grandmother, mother and brother. We were holding each others' hands. A strong golden energy flowed between us. By and by, all my relatives on my mother's side joined us, women and men, even my former deceased husband, my godson and his daughter. We were dancing around a tree, singing and sending love to one another. I felt a very strong and happy feeling.

After this journey, I went off to our Morningstar Astral Temple. I travelled in the Merkabah and went right into a reflecting pool when I arrived. Everywhere in the temple there was a huge, very brilliant light: a living being without boundaries formed by light. Suddenly the pool extended into a lake that lay outside the temple, lined by high, snow-covered mountains. It was dark night with many stars in the black sky. I looked up to the sky and felt the Star Goddess's presence. Some of the stars fell down into my gown as golden coins, similar to the Grimms' fairytale of "Sterntaler." Someone whispered "health and wealth" out of the sky. I had a strong feeling of abundance.

Whenever I succeed in connecting with the Star Goddess and Her universe, I'm at ease, integrated, and full of power in my Morningstar and shamanic work.

Demons
(Internal and External)

One month later, at the time of June New Moon, I had three dreams in two subsequent nights that helped me to see my internal demons. Our external demons are at the same time partly internal, and vice versa. In their "external" shape, they can be identified more easily. I find it much harder to recognize the internal ones.

The internal demons I named at that time are fear of failure, overwork, fear of not being good enough, fear of losing myself in an "ocean of sad feelings," and fear of being rejected by those who are afraid of strong(-headed) women.

In the category of external demons, my dreams were occupied by different types of men. Some of these men really existed, some were archetypes. These men included a close friend and partner who had turned away from me when he met a woman who seemed weak enough to make him feel strong. This happened 40 years ago, but in my dream I could feel the pain as I had then. I saw a middle-aged man and a big male pig—my father—in my house, bullying me and trying to stop me from attending my beloved cats. The third demon I encountered was a husband—thank Goddess, one that had nothing to do with my real life—who was the owner of several brothels. In my dream I had been a play-mate in one of these brothels before I became his obedient wife. I succeeded in unmasking him and destroying his sex imperium with the help of a young woman, my alter ego.

Apart from this young woman, there were two male allies in my three dreams who helped me to overcome my feelings of helplessness, hatred and fury: my godson Alex and my cat Fritzchen. Alex helped me to step back in my dreams and look at what happened, clear-sighted; Fritzchen showed me a mark on his body, a circle with a dot in the middle—the symbol for "Sun." Fritzchen helped me to connect with my inner sun, which was strong but overshadowed and partly darkened by fury, hatred and feelings of impotence.

In this intensive phase of dreaming, shamanic and astral journeys in May and June 2012, I realized that I had been doing demon work before it became a homework theme, and the Morningstar work had initiated even more demon work.

Visions

Sometimes, when I visit the Morningstar Astral Temple during New Moons, I have experiences that, from my point of view, are visions of the future and present time.

October 2011

There was a long staircase behind the temple door, lined with people dressed in white: they bowed to me and I bowed to them when I climbed the stairs. At the end of the stairs, I found a round seat with golden walls, like a bowl. The Peacock God was there, spreading his tail like a wheel. I was invited to climb into the seat, which was the Black Heart associated with Center. I grew smaller so that I could comfortably sit in the seat together with the Peacock. He welcomed me and asked if I was ready to go on a journey to some of his worlds. I agreed, and he said "Fasten your seat belt." We took off. First, we came across overwhelming light that caused me to close my eyes. This light was the gown of the Star Goddess. I felt absolutely safe and at home. We saw stars being born and dying, like extra-terrestrial fireworks, and colored lights like the Aurora Borealis. We came to a pale ball, a moon. This did not look inviting. The Peacock said "Look at the other side of the moon." There were big holes, fire weapons being shot at the moon's surface and back into space: the home of hatred. The Peacock said, "That's where people live who worship nothing else but hatred. They are so attracted by hatred that they automatically come here after death, but they have a choice. It's their own decision to live in hatred; they could leave and go to some other place at any time. Mind you, they are always in the hands of God Herself, wherever they are." We saw Earth, still blue but sweating and groaning. The surrounding atmosphere was badly hurt and unstable in several places. The Great Spider Woman was weaving a web to stabilize Earth, but

I could not see what happened to people and other living beings on Earth.

The Peacock said, "It's time to return to the temple." We sailed back in our "Black Heart" seat. The Peacock disappeared into his orange and lemon garden. I descended the staircase and took a bath in the pool, where I found there were two swans, black and white, and pink dolphins. I swam with them and felt relaxed. I saw people I knew from my cohort: Helena feeding a lion in the Peacock's orange garden, Anareetta riding a horse at a gallop, Nikolai standing by the altar singing an opera aria praising a God/Goddess, a man I did not know with a small child on his knees, and Thorn dressed in black and silver practicing magic with her wand on the left side of the temple. I wished them well and left through the front door.

After this journey and even now when I remember, I had a strong feeling of having seen the present state of our planet from a detached point of view. The Great Spider Woman plays an important part in the change the Earth is going through now. This reminds me of some very old myths in the traditions of native Americans that looked upon Spider Woman as the creative power behind existence. An Australian myth suggests that Earth will not collapse if Spider Woman keeps on weaving her web. In northern, central and southern European mythology, there are the trias of the three Norns who represent the

Goddesses of fate and who are mistresses of the past, present and future of everything that lives.

December 2012

I started from my home, on my shamanic dream path on which I climb a rainbow that leads me to the top of a nearby hill, the Steinkopf. I found a clearing with a fire in the middle. All of my shamanic allies were assembled in a round, sitting on stone seats like thrones. They greeted me warmly but seriously and said, "You are late in these times of total change." The elements came across me. Fire and water lifted me up; earth dug me in; and air swirled me around. I was accepted, and everything was okay.

All of them knew that I wanted to visit the Morningstar Astral Temple. We all mounted the Merkabah. I felt slightly embarrassed, but my owl Pallas and I shape-shifted, and I felt at ease. The temple was a huge rosy bubbling half of a ball with golden ornaments, like a tent. Inside was a horrible scene: a young woman being whipped and raped by three men. I flew to her in the shape of my owl and touched the men with my wing. They let the young woman alone and shrank immediately to grains of sand in the dust. The woman flew up: she was the Goddess Lilith. She embraced Pallas and we flew away.

My other allies remained to attend hundreds and thousands of women who came there from all parts of the Earth and from all times. The women bathed in the temple pool, received soothing treatment by my allies, and showed each other their mutual respect and love. The whole scene vibrated with well-being, smelling and sounding like paradise. The women gave birth to children who had never known the past time of hatred between the sexes and were able to start a new age.

Lilith and Pallas left the protective tent of the temple and met the Great Spider Woman, who held the temple in her web. We flew down to Earth. Everywhere we went, the world changed: women freed themselves from impotence and dependence. They trusted and helped each other, and by doing so broke the neck of patriarchy. Lilith and Pallas flew to Mekka, and the black cover of the Kaaba was washed away. Lilith took her place as the great Goddess she had been in this part of the world. She stood atop the stone cube. Women rejoiced and men fell on their knees and worshipped her. She and Pallas flew to Sinai. In the middle of the desert was a black cloud that held the essence of the past age of patriarchal order. Warlords of the patriarchal God protected this essence. Lilith came down and swallowed the black cloud, digested it, and left a heap of camel dung. The dung dried in the desert and shepherds used it for their fire. The power of patriarchal suppressors was gone for good. Everywhere Lilith and Pallas came along, women shook off their yoke to aid and love each other. The Great Spider Woman lent them a hand and spread her web over patriarchal countries, until the women in these countries had freed themselves. Europe was the focus of these changes. Here were many centres from which these revolutions emerged.

Lilith, Pallas, and Great Spider Woman worked hand in hand, wing in hand, and leg in hand until the world had changed completely. This was the last minute for survival on Earth.

Lilith and Pallas returned to the Astral Temple. The Great Spider Woman still holds the Earth and the temple in her web. Lilith rested in a hang-mat between two palm trees. She was cradled by a soft wind and lit by a mild sun. Women from all parts of the world and all times kept coming to the temple. Pallas called my allies together, and we went back to the Steinkopf in the Merkabah. We found a big party: golden seats arranged around the fire. Women I had known in the Goddess Movement and those I know now were there, all laughing, singing, dancing, eating and drinking. They appreciated each others' presence, rejoiced, and greeted the new age. Pallas and I separated and I went back home along my shamanic dream path.

Happy New Age!

1–9

by Sophia Bonnie Wodin

#1

> A place in each soul
> knows its uniqueness.
> Therein lies a gift
> that completes the world.

#2

> Gently, tenderly
> move into the day.
> Sensations creep up the body
> delight to stretch,
> meeting what comes.
>
> Like the dawn,
> I eagerly await

what arises now,
and now,
and now.

#3

The small one lodged
deeply in the belly
like a marsupial,
climbs blind
towards the heart
seeking nourishment.
There she nestles into
comfort.

The air is rosy-gold.

#4

Behind closed eyes
cloud banks gather.

Tumbling over boulders
merging and separating,
merging again.
Moving ever
towards the Sea.

The heart lifts
awareness
in this exact moment.

And breath regains
balance.

Water and Fire and Air
return to Earth.
Once again.

#5

There is something in the soul
that lives in the heart.
Something that overcomes
the conditioned mind
and connects with
the expanded mind.

It is called the power to Dare.
It aligns us with our soul's purpose.

#6

In the greening of this world,
in the rising of the sun,
in the shining of the smile,
in the comfort of the arm,
in the gentle of the word,
in the fleeting of the kiss,
in the honoring of the soul,
in the opening of the heart:

Beltane blessings abound!

#7

    When I feel you,
    nestled in the hallows
    of my heart,
    tenderness
    bubbles up
    like a spring
    emerging
    from the depths
    of the Mother.

#8

    When your heart lies heavy
    and your sweet body yearns
    for touch
    when there is no one of this world
    to hold you,
    remember
    the Good Green Earth holds
    Her children.

    So call out with your
    laden heart.
    Speak the words that need
    no sound.
    She will hear you.
    Lean into
    The Mother.

#9

Sweet Goddess

your presence near

in the essence of each rose.

Draw into my heart

and there

bloom.

Pronounced

by Brian C

His name was Al. He was 84 years old. He had several different careers in his time, but he retired years ago. He had a minor bout with cancer during middle age, and beat it.

He liked to talk shop about e-books and his new Kindle. He used Facebook to keep in contact with his kids, and grandkids, and great-grandkids. He spent a lot time walking, and fishing, and keeping up his lawn. He didn't eat very much but he usually felt pretty good.

Last week he came to the hospital because he was a little short of breath. The ER did an ultrasound, an X-ray, and a CT. These scans showed fluid on his lung, and possible other issues. Our surgeons did a thoracotomy and placed a chest tube.

When he got to my floor, he was very weak but in good spirits. His respirations sounded awful, but he was breathing okay with just a little bit of supplemental oxygen. The chest tube was draining fluid and his lung was re-expanding. He couldn't move much without assistance, but he put in as much effort as he could manage. He told jokes about all the wires and lines we had him hooked up to. He had no appetite but drank the nutrient shakes we gave him for supplements.

This weekend, the pathology results from his biopsy came back. The physicians explained that his cancer had come back, aggressively. This time it had spread to his lungs. Chemotherapy might work, as it did last time, but the chances were poor. Radiation was not an option. Surgery was impossible.

Al took this better than anyone could expect. He was a bit withdrawn, afterward, but he still told jokes. He forced a laugh and said that he beat cancer once before, and dammit, he'd do it again. He seemed to need more company. He found lots of reasons to call me into the room, and keep me there for a while. I didn't mind. I often had some free time during my shift. I spent a lot of it there, just talking with him.

A few nights ago, while we were chatting in the very wee hours, Al suddenly sat up on the side of his bed. He pulled off his oxygen cannula, tossed it on the floor, and started disconnecting his cardiac monitor leads. It was the most movement I'd ever seen him do without help. He said, "Get this shit off me. I know I'm a dead man. I might as well be comfortable."

I explained that we would not do anything he didn't want us to do. If he wanted us to withdraw care, and make him as comfortable as possible, then I would call the physicians and get those orders. But didn't he want to talk to his family first? Would he please, just for now, let me put his oxygen and his monitor back on, so he could be comfortable while we made the arrangements?

He agreed. I got him back in bed and wired back up to the monitor. Then I excused myself and started making phone calls.

The arrangements weren't complete by the time my shift ended. I made sure the next nurse was aware of Al's wishes, and was on top of what needed to be done. Before I left for the day, I went back in to his room, and promised him that we were doing what he wanted.

That day, while I slept, the orders went in. The whole team of physicians spoke with him, in person, in pairs and small groups, going over the exact details of his prognosis and his options. He chose to be placed on comfort care only. His whole family came in to visit. Some of those tried to change his mind. Others just came to say goodbye. There was a large family conference about where Al would live now, for hospice care, once he was discharged from the hospital.

His youngest great-granddaughter brought in a poster she had made from a blown-up photograph, of the two of them together, carrying fishing rods over their shoulders. Surrounding the photo were stick drawings of fish and boats and waves. Across the top, in fat blue crayon, childish handwriting said "Get Well Soon."

By the time I came back in the evening, Al didn't look at all well. He had refused to take any breathing treatments all day, or most other medications either. He was pale, and gasping. His oxygen was turned up as high as it could go, without using a cumbersome mask that he didn't want. He didn't respond to questions. His daughter, the only family member still at the hospital, thought he seemed to be pain.

I gave morphine to relieve air hunger. I gave lorazepam to relieve anxiety. I turned on a fan in the room to provide a sensation of easier air movement. I turned off the cardiac monitor and removed the electrodes. I disconnected the IV. I washed his face, and remade his bed, and turned down the lights. He appeared at last calm, and comfortable. His daughter kissed him goodbye, and left to take care of the rest of her family.

Once he was alone I checked on him every ten minutes. Only a few rounds later—less than an hour—I came in and noted that his breathing was agonal, in a distinctive pattern of sudden gasps. As I watched, he took one more breath, and then no more.

I checked for a pulse on the radial artery, in his wrist. Then the carotid, in his neck. No blood stirred under my fingertips.

I put my stethoscope on his chest and heard faint sounds. Not the two part lub-dub, lub-dub of a functional heart, but a soft single tick, tick, tick, just electrical twitching, too weak to flex the heart or open the valves. As I listened, the tick slowed like a clock winding down, and finally it ceased.

I found another nurse to listen and confirm my assessment.

I pronounced a man dead.

Bridghid 2013

by Sophia Bonnie Wodin

Do you hear Her
whispering in your ear,
inspiration flowing,
stirring your imagination
with the song of your soul
as She sweeps
Her mantle
over home and field?

Do you feel Her
tap tapping in your heart
at Her forge,
hammering raw desire
into aligned Will?

Do you know Her
washing your feet
with the sacred waters
of her living well,
opening you to
becoming,
casting doubt
from your heart?

She comes
with the quickening
of the year,
heralding
the quickening
of our lives.

Listen with your heart
your bones
your belly.

Brighid arises
emerging from depth,
turning the Wheel

Towards Spring.

Fragment: Godsoul to Me

by Ariana Dawnhawk

when you forget
i will be there
in your feet solid on the ground
my hand on your back
my voice in your ear
stand up straight my love
for I know who you are

My Demon, My Self

by Kathy Nance

I had not expected the fear.

Fear in a gut-clenching knot. Fear beneath the bristling bravado. Fear that shrieked, "Leave me alone! Let me be! Don't come near me!"

Fear was the Demon's fuel, after all. Fear tied in knots, knots that had been used to whip my self-esteem for years. The fear that I am not special, fear that I have no gift worth offering to the world, fear that if I do dare to offer my creativity, no one will want it. No one will be interested.

And we do live in a culture that encourages this fear. For if everyone can publish, then what is special about any one publication? If anyone can put art up online, how does any one piece break through? What difference does it make whether I offer anything, or not, if there are millions of offerings available? Why is mine special?

It was an exercise at one of our Morningstar advanced student retreats that gave me the insight into my Demon's fuel. We'd been working with the idea that behind the knotted-up complexes of issues that kept us from becoming whole was a personal Demon. To help us get a better feel for what drove our Demons, we worked in pairs. Each member of the pair took a turn embodying the personal Demon, then the Godsoul. The Godsoul, or Holy Guardian Angel, or Sacred Dove, is that part of each one of us that connects to the Divine.

The second major insight: when I held the space of the Godsoul and confronted the Demon, all I felt was love. And compassion for its fear. And attraction—yes, attraction—to its energy. "Oh, I could really create something with all that energy! Don't be afraid. Don't hide. You're beautiful," my Divine Self said to the Demon across from me.

And it was the same for many of us—the feeling that the Demon, the stumbling block, was afraid of the Divine Light we carried. And that it wanted to hide.

Coaxing a Demon into laying down its sovereignty, though, was not nearly so easy. It took months to trace the cords back, and back. Each time I thought I had found the Chief Demon that held the reins of a team of lessers, there was a bigger and badder Demon issue at its back. I finally found the team leader at the core of my Demon

My Demon, My Self

Complex at a retreat for advanced students not only of Morningstar but of three other Schools. I had been feeling very insignificant there. I felt like everyone else was more magickally adept, more firm in daily practice, more advanced in spiritual connection, more psychically sensitive. I felt that the teachers could see right through me, and wondered why I'd been invited to attend. And then I knew.

This feeling of "Not Being Special" was so familiar. So obvious. It was like the Tarot card in the Celtic cross that "covers" a querant: that which is so close to our face that we can't see it at all.

And so, the process of working with the Demon began anew. I spent a month sitting in meditation with it. I drew a triangle with words of power around it, filled in the Name I had give the Demon in its center. I went in mediation to my personal place of power, confronted the Demon there. With a whip, I snapped off its crown. We spoke. It combusted, became small.

At Yule, I burned the triangle containing its name. I watched the flames flare, sparks flying upward, as the paper was consumed. I was ready for a new beginning.

And yet—the Demon lingered. Others have found this as well. Because the demon, sadly, is not a magical being that can be summoned and banished in a Goetic fashion. It is a part of us, a thought pattern woven into our cerebral network. It must be teased out and unknotted by rites of unbinding. It must be given new tasks, new work to do. The neural networks that house it must be rerouted.

I remember seeing the artist Sark at a book signing. She gave her self-sabotaging parts fun jobs like "go to Madagascar, find new lemur species." I first gave my Demon sentry duty, having it look out for danger. It loved that, and grew a bit stronger. Next, I gave my Demon the job of cheering on my accomplishments. It was like putting Gollum in a cheerleader's outfit. It was not amused and did a terrible job.

I then tried simply conversing with it—telling it that it no longer can be in charge. That instead of Absolute Monarch, it had the job of sitting with the Loyal Opposition. That is, that it might not agree with the policies that had my larger self heading towards a more creative and visible path, but that it had the responsibility to support that goal as best it could.

I'm basing this on the teachings of Trebbe Johnson, who said that each of us has a part that is like a sentry, that looks for trouble and tries to keep us safe. Unfortunately, it can try too hard to keep us safe, and instead keep us from taking the kinds of risks we need to take in order to grow.

I thought of my Grandma Wright. I loved her, of course. And in some ways, she was fearless. I'd seen her take the head off a snake with a hoe, or dispatch a mouse in the kitchen with a swat of her sensible shoe. She'd faced down the Great Depression, three wars, crop failures. And maybe that's why she was always expecting the worst. Any happy plan for the future would be greeted by warnings that the desired outcome might not happen.

And she was right—things go wrong. And it's good to have a Plan B. But if all we do is obsess about what can go wrong, then nothing new gets tried.

I learned after my Grandpa Wright died that she regretted not taking a chance. She and Grandpa, when young, had wanted to go from church to church singing and preaching. He had a guitar that I'd never heard him play. I don't know when he stopped. I know he dropped out of minister's training to help his family on the farm in the 1920s. She said they shouldn't have let that stop them; they should have set out and toured those little country churches.

Given the way Grandpa could command a room, the lack of a diploma would have been no obstacle. They could have had a marvelous time. But they did the sensible thing. They stayed on the farm, took in Grandma's younger brother to raise, brought up children of their own. Grandma let the Demon win.

She passed on that fear. What prompted that memory was finding a piece of homework from our long,

Morningstar process of demon work. Thorn had asked us to do an exercise from *Kissing the Limitless*. In that, we write a "family taboo" on an index card. Then, we respond to the taboo on the back of the card. And enclose it in a thank-you card. On the card, we write thanks to the taboo for serving a purpose during part of our life, and bid it farewell. A friend mails the card when the time seems right.

I had been cleaning, and picked up a card that had fallen, forgotten, from my night table. It said. "Don't get too big." That was what Grandma said when I would tell her, as a child, of my plans for the future. Or speak confidently about my abilities. "Don't get too big" was her way of correcting what she saw as either the sin of Pride, or perhaps of trying to shield an imaginative, bright, artistically confident child and teenager from a world that she hadn't had the confidence to challenge. And that she feared would disappoint and trample me as well.

Try as I might to struggle against it, I realized I had internalized that taboo as part of my "I have nothing special to offer" Chief Demon. And it was time to stop.

So I told my Demon that story. And said that I wanted it to help me look out for danger, to point out where I could use a Plan B. But that was it. No ruling. No keeping me down on the farm with fear. Instead, it was to use that alertness to help me become more excellent. To use awareness of a plan's flaws, or a project's shortcomings, to become stronger and better. To shore them up, not let them keep me down.

It's still an uneasy alliance, and there are times when the fear does win. But not nearly so often as before. Now, when we talk, I don't feel that hard, cold knot of fear I did when we first locked eyes. No, I can feel love, and compassion, and an eager attraction to use its energy. Not wholly Demon, not wholly Godsoul. A blend of both. Myself.

The Merkabah

by Sophia Bonnie Wodin

Of synchronicity I sing.
Yesterday's yard sale find
becomes the chariot
of tomorrow.
The God's smile
marks our way.

Oh, great unfolding!
Oh, path of becoming
and you of liberation!
Meet you here,
in the heart
of the matter.
For here stands
Beauty!

Liberation seeks
the limitless.
And becoming seeks the
ground
Where each flows
light expands
transforming
all it touches.

And what be
Beauty
I ask you,
if not
the human
Heart?

– 6 February 2013

Contributor Biographies

Allyson Ramage is inspired by wild beauty, balance, mothering, and spirituality. Her creative expressions are a celebration of movement and life through dance, the written word, and the visual arts. Performing throughout California and New York, she has worked with three modern dance companies throughout her career: Isaacs, McCaleb, and Dancers; Strong Current; and Huckabay McAllister Dance. She feels honored to have a painting included in this anthology. Her website is www.allysonramage.com.

Annette Rath-Beckmann was born on August 1, 1951, in Bielefeld, Germany. She runs a "School for Matriarchal Shamanism—UDAGAN" (www.udagan.de) and lives in a small village in the middle of Germany, near the Meißner mountain, a prominent mythological place of the ancient Goddess Holle.

At the Georg August University Goettingen, she studied history, early medieval English and philosophy, and was head of the State and University Library Bremen in her professional life.

In 2006, she joined Thorn's Feri, then Morningstar, training and integrates Morningstar magic in her shamanic work and vice versa. Two of her recent publications deal with the outstanding role of female shamanism in paleolithic and neolithic times in Europe (www.udagan.de/Annette-die Gründerin/Publikationen).

Anthony Rella is a witch, psychotherapist, and writer living in beautiful Seattle, Washington, with his husband and dog. His work has been included in the Scarlet Imprint anthology *Mandragora* and Minor Arcana's *Ghosts in the Gaslight, Monsters in Steam*. Anthony has been studying with Thorn since 2006. He keeps a blog at his professional site, www.anthonyrella.com.

Ariana Dawnhawk has been studying with Thorn for the past eight years. She works to open the way and holds space for others to teach, learn, and stand in their power. She enjoys and practices many forms of creativity.

Brian C has been studying with Thorn and Morningstar since 2007. When he started he was a computer programmer, and thought he was happy enough with that career. But this training helps develop insight, and he came to realize that he was not really satisfied with his office job. The training also develops a powerful set of emotional and spiritual tools, and he found he was motivated to use those tools for something more demanding and of more lasting impact. In 2009 he decided to quit his office job and go to nursing school.

He is now a registered nurse and works in a small city in the Midwest. At the time he met the patient he writes about, Brian was a staff RN in a hospital critical care unit, providing care to the most seriously ill patients.

Ealasaid A. Haas is a technical writer by day and a bookbinder, Aikido student, blogger, movie reviewer, knitter, gamer, and gardener by night. She, her partner, and their two cats live in the Pacific Northwest, having recently escaped from the San Francisco Bay Area. She has been a practicing pagan since 1996, a student of T. Thorn Coyle since 2006, and part of Morningstar Mystery School almost since its inception.

Elfin would love nothing more than to sit down and have a cup of tea with you. There's something amazing at the heart of every person, something that calls to be seen, heard and known; making that connection is at the heart of E's work.

Fortuna is an American witch who has been living in the Netherlands since 2003. Her "magickal DNA" includes a stubborn streak of mysticism that the suburbs of Los Angeles, where she was born, just could not dilute. A lifelong seeker in various magickal and mystical traditions, Fortuna is an initiate of the Anderson Feri Tradition. A student of T. Thorn Coyle since 2005, Fortuna holds Blue and White cords in Morningstar Mystery School (MStar), and has acted as a Mentor for the School. She has had the extraordinary luck of teaching and priestessing Reclaiming-style witchcraft at workshops and Witchcamps in Europe and the UK since 2007. She works one-on-one and in groups to help magickal people of every type—witch and shaman, cunning person and magician—in their development. As a lifelong student, she continues to develop her own magickal knowledge with teachers from various streams, to work as a divinatrix and Tarot counselor, and to create poetry, chants, and art to honour God in all Hir faces.

Kathy Nance writes from a Midwestern suburb near the Missouri River. Her Paganism has its origins in long horseback rides through the Illinois woods with her grandfather and tending gardens with her grandmothers. She took their lessons of the natural world's cycles and our cooperative place in it and went looking for the Divine

Contributor Biographies

there as well. Her current spiritual practice is informed by her advanced-level studies with Morningstar Mystery School, in which she holds the Blue and White cords of self-mastery and psychic skills. She leaves offerings to the Fey and to her ancestors, as well as a multi-ethnic family of Gods and Goddesses who so far are content to share altar space. She also has long-standing but manageable feng shui, tarot and astrological addictions. She adds to that mix insights from readings in anthropology, sociology, philosophy, world mythologies and history.

She has a B.S. with majors in mass communications, sociology and English. She has worked as a newspaper education reporter, feature writer and editor. Her freelance work has been published in general circulation and specialty publications in the U.S. and Great Britain. Her blog, *Gateway Goddess,* can be found on the Pagan portal of the interfaith site Patheos.com. Before coming to Patheos, she was a featured writer for Civil Religion, the *St. Louis Post-Dispatch* interfaith blog. She has organized both large and small public Pagan celebrations, bringing together groups from a variety of traditions in the St. Louis area. She can also be found sharing opinions on Facebook and on Twitter, @GatewayGoddess.

Kevin Faulkner has been T. Thorn Coyle's student since the sychronicity train unambiguously delivered Kevin to

Thorn's tutelage in 2007. The years before and since, which Kevin has spent in solitary practice and study of magic and astrology on the red plains of Oklahoma and the roads and forests of America from coast to coast, have formed a unique and personal practice for growth and change informed by extensive studies in history, anthropology, philosophy, and religious and gender studies. Kevin seeks to marry his rigorous intellectual and spiritual training to taste and renew the transformative well springs of magic behind the western esoteric traditions that they may flow forth healing to a culture in psychic crisis.

Kevin also enjoys gardening, herbal medicine, dance, mandolin and travel. Kevin recently set aside life as a nomad to help found a Radical Faerie artists' housing compound in West Oakland.

Litha is a poet, mother, grandmother, gardener, dancer, lover and witch. She is a former student in the Morningstar Mystery School and has greatly appreciated her work with Thorn Coyle and other Morningstar students.

Lyssa Heartsong (Kelly Grejda) is a wild goth girl newly transplanted from the east coast to the west coast. She currently resides in Oakland, CA, and spends her time writing poetry, painting, spinning yarn, and making jewelry. The fruits of her fairytale superpowers can be found at www.etsy.com/shop/heartsongglamourie.

Nikolai has studied with Morning Star for more than 7 years and also has a background in Huna.

He loves dancing, drumming and writing, and lives with his family in northern Germany.

Rynn Fox is a Witch, priest and mystic who has been active in the Pagan community since 1997. She is one of the three founders of Coru Cathubodua, a priesthood dedicated to the ancient Irish Goddess the Morrigan, and currently serves as their Communications Officer helping to champion the virtues of sovereignty, honor, and personal responsibility. She is a longtime, continuing student of Morningstar Mystery School and holds the Blue and White cords of self-mastery and psychic skills. A Feri practitioner, she has studied with Karina Blackheart and continues to study with T. Thorn Coyle. She is also a staff writer for Pagan and minority religion media outlet, The Wild Hunt (www.wildhunt.org).

Sean McMahon is a visual artist and writer who lives in Oakland. His first encounter with magic was with his mother's Rider-Waite deck at the age of eight, and he has been drawn to exploring the intersections of gnosis, spiritual practice and art ever since. He is a student of

Morningstar Mystery School and a member of the 2014 Dustbunnies online class, taught by Valerie Walker.

Sophia Bonnie Wodin works with people of all ages, genders and traditions to support each individual's journey to wholeness.

Woven throughout Sophia's work are diverse strands, including psycho-therapeutic training (M.Ed, Lesley University, 1977), Buddhist mindfulness practice (since 1978), and Goddess-oriented, Earth-Centered spiritual practices (since 1988). Sophia's background also includes Reiki level two, conscious communication training, and conflict resolution. Gathering the strands of these varied teachings and practices, Sophia has arrived at a continually unfolding, unique relationship with spirit.

Sophia developed the 13-month Priestessing Your Life Training based on the belief that we each have the ability to travel our soul's journey with grace, wisdom and competence. Using the four ancient powers—To Know, To Will, To Dare and To Choose Silence—we awaken to the power and purpose of our life's purpose.

Her Writer's Circles, which open to new participants in January, April and September, focus on aspects of spirituality including The Voice of the Feminine Divine; our relationship with the land; deep ecology, and more. She also offers day-long writing retreats to deepen the work.

www.ingramcontent.com/pod-product-compliance
Lightning Source LLC
LaVergne TN
LVHW091255080426
835510LV00007B/276